Dynamic Cover Letters
for New Graduates

Dynamic Cover Letters
for New Graduates

Katharine Hansen

Ten Speed Press
Berkeley, California

Ten Speed Press
P.O. Box 7123
Berkeley, California 94707
www.tenspeed.com

Distributed in Australia by Simon and Schuster Australia, in Canada by Ten Speed Press Canada, in New Zealand by Southern Publishers Group, in South Africa by Real Books, in Southeast Asia by Berkeley Books, and in the United Kingdom and Europe by Airlift Book Company.

Cover design by Fifth Street Design
Text design by Jeff Brandenburg/Image Comp

Library of Congress Cataloging-in-Publication Data

Hansen, Katharine.
        Dynamic cover letters for new graduates/Katharine Hansen.
            p.   cm.
        ISBN 0-89815-984-9 (alk. paper)
        1. Cover letters.   2. College graduates—Employment.   I. Title
        HF5383.H278 1998   97-51729
        808'.06665—dc21   CIP

First printing, 1998
Printed in the United States of America

3 4 5 6 7 8 9 10 — 05 04 03 02 01

Contents

Introduction x

Part One: The Cover Letter's Role in a New Graduate's Job Search 1

Securing the Interview 2

Using the Cover Letter to Differentiate Yourself from
More Experienced Job-Seekers 4

Your Unique Selling Proposition 4

The PEP (Profitability, Efficiency, Productivity) Formula. 7

Quantify and Exemplify. 8

The Three Types of Cover Letters. 9

Cover Letter Structure 12

The Three Most Common Cover Letter Mistakes . . . and
How to Avoid Them 14

How to Make the Employer Sit Up and Take Notice 20

The Academic Frame of Reference: Don't Let It Overwhelm Your Letter. . . 24

What to Include—and What Not To 27

Writing and Editing with Finesse 31

Standard Business Letter Format 33

Packaging and Mailing. 36

Part Two: The Top Ten Ways New Grads Can Write Can't-Miss, Dynamic Cover Letters................................... 41

Making the Most of Your College Experience 42

Emphasizing Your Transferable Work Experience and Skills............. 48

Crafting Enticing Openers.. 54

Accentuating the Positive 57

Closing the Sale with a Proactive Final Paragraph.................... 60

Emphasizing What You Can Do for the Employer.................... 61

Demonstrating Knowledge of the Company and Industry............. 64

Tailoring Your Letter to a Want Ad 68

Networking Your Way to Irresistible Cover Letters.................. 73

Sharpening Your Focus.. 77

Part Three: Sample Letters for Special Situations 81

Internships, Externships, and Summer Jobs 82

Requesting Informational Interviews 95

Letters to Your College Career Placement Office 98

Letters to Recruiters Coming to Your Campus..................... 100

Letters Sent Without Resumes 103

Follow-Up Letters 105

    The All-Important Thank-You Letter........................ 105

    Following Up After Rejection............................... 112

    The What-Did-I-Do-Wrong Letter 113

    Letter to Accept a Job Offer 114

    Letter to Decline an Offer 114

Graduate School Application Letters 115

Part Four: Sending Your Cover Letter into Cyberspace: The Internet Job Hunt.................................. 119

Six Ways to Use Your Cover Letter on the Internet................. 120

    Taking Advantage of Resume Databases...................... 120

    Responding to Online Ads................................. 121

    Using the ResumePATH Web Site........................... 121

    Creating Your Own Web Page.............................. 122

    Responding to Print Ads with E-Mail 122

    Posting Your Cover Letter to a Usenet Newsgroup.............. 122

Part Five: Sample Letters for New Grads Seeking Today's Hottest Jobs 125

English 126
Foreign Languages 127
Philosophy 128
Psychology 129
Sociology 130
Religious Studies 131
International Relations 132
History 133
Political Science 134
Geography 135
Visual Arts 136
Graphic Design 137
Performing Arts 138
Elementary Education 139
Secondary Education 140
Biology 141
Chemistry 142
Biochemistry 143
Agricultural Science 144
Math 145
Physics 146
Chemical Engineering 147
Mechanical Engineering 148
Health 149
Exercise Science 150
Computer Science 151
Management Information Systems 152
Information Technology 153
Business 154
International Business 155
Management 156
Marketing 157
Finance 158
Accounting 159
Public Relations 160
Communications 161

Part Six: Letters for Graduate and Professional School Grads 163
    Letters for Law School Graduates 164
    Letters for Graduates of Other Professional and Graduate Schools 166

Resources 173

Index 175

About the Author 179

This book is dedicated to all my students at Stetson University, past, present, and future.

I would also like to acknowledge the contributions of the many college students and new graduates who submitted cover letters for critiquing, providing invaluable research for this book and models for many of the sample cover letters herein.

I especially thank my partner, Randall S. Hansen, for his support, wisdom, patience, and unfailingly priceless advice. You not only encouraged me to fly solo, but were the wind beneath my wings.

For information about having your cover letter critiqued, write or e-mail:

Katharine Hansen

1250 Valley View Lane

DeLand, FL 32720-2364

E-mail: khansen@stetson.edu

or visit this site on the World Wide Web:

http: www.stetson.edu/~rhansen/dcl.html

Introduction

While college students have always been an important audience for my previous book, *Dynamic Cover Letters*, written with my partner, Randall S. Hansen, it was not until I began teaching college students regularly that I realized the extent to which you, the college student, have distinct needs in your search for employment.

Job-search correspondence is an important element of the business communication class I teach at Stetson University in DeLand, Florida. Through my teaching, I have become increasingly aware of how difficult it is for college students to craft effective resumes and cover letters when they have comparatively little work experience. While it is true that more and more college students are taking advantage of experiential learning opportunities—internships, summer jobs, co-op jobs—they must still compete in the job market with candidates who have more experience, and with other college students. How do you make yourself stand out? How do you compel an employer to look at your resume? How do you get them to call you for an interview?

You can write a dynamic cover letter. This book will show you how.

You'll learn to make the most of your college experience in your cover letter, which is especially important if you have little or no work experience. You'll learn how to play up your transferable and applicable skills, portraying them as exquisitely applicable to your post-college career. You'll see how to make your letter so appealing that the employer won't be able to put it down. You'll discover how to project the enthusiasm and confidence that make college students so attractive to employers. You'll master the art of closing the sale by asking for an interview at the end of your letter. You will understand how to paint an irresistible picture of what you will do for the employer's company. This book also teaches you the little-used but effective technique of showcasing your knowledge of the employer's company. It shows you how to write a sharply focused cover letter targeted to a want ad. It teaches you to parlay networking skills into a particularly powerful type of cover letter and demonstrates how to deploy your cover letter as part of a job search on the Internet.

You'll find more than sixty samples of cover letters written by real college students and new graduates who have used them successfully. These samples are especially meant for use by college students. And *Dynamic Cover Letters for New*

Graduates offers twelve sample letters for students seeking internships and summer jobs, along with numerous letters for special situations and dozens of excerpts from great student letters.

I've crafted this book with the needs of my own students in mind. I'm confident that this book will not only enhance their success at writing effective and dynamic cover letters, but will also raise their comfort level and make the prospect of their first major job search a little less traumatic. It's my intention that this book will do the same for you. Congratulations on your upcoming or recent graduation; I wish you much success in your job hunt!

— KATHARINE HANSEN

PART ONE

The Cover Letter's Role in a New Graduate's Job Search

In a very real sense, the term "cover letter" has deviated from its original meaning. The letter's main purpose used to be to "cover" the resume and explain why you were sending your resume to the employer. Today the cover letter can do much more; in fact, many employers say they attach more importance to the cover letter than to the resume. Part One explains that the cover letter plays a major role in getting you an interview—and since very few people are hired sight unseen, landing the interview is key to receiving a job offer. This part of the book also describes some of the special challenges—and opportunities—that college students have in their search for employment.

Securing the Interview

Since college career services offices often emphasize resumes over cover letters, it may come as a rude shock when you have to write a cover letter for the first time. In fact, many—if not most—college students truly struggle to write cover letters. They don't know where to begin, what to include, or how to make it sound right. Putting the cover letter in its proper perspective can help.

True or False: A good cover letter can get you a job.

False. While a good cover letter can certainly help you land a job, its main purpose is not to get you a job, but to get you an interview. Obtaining an interview is crucial to getting a job. Every effective direct-mail sales letter tries to close the sale by motivating the recipient to take a specific action, and a cover letter should work the same way. It's a direct-mail sales letter that should close the sale by asking for an interview. You'll see words to this effect again in these pages, but they bear repeating because they are important. It's critical that you see your cover letter as an opportunity to close the sale by asking for an interview. The biggest reason it's so important to close the sale? Because surprisingly few job-seekers do so. If you do, you will have a clear advantage over other job-seekers who sit back and hope the employer contacts them. You'll see more about this in "Closing the Sale," page 60.

Of course, your cover letter has other purposes, too:

- A cover letter should tell the employer what type of position you want. Even when you respond to an employment ad, it's not always obvious what position a cover letter is responding to, especially if you're writing to a large company with many openings. When you're sending your cover letter uninvited by an ad, it's especially important to tell the employer what kind of job you seek.

- A good cover letter should make the reader want to learn more about you by reading your resume. A cover letter should give an employer a broad and inviting overview of your qualifications, but it is your resume that contains the specifics. Your cover letter and resume should work in tandem.

- Your cover letter can provide or expand upon a resume element that is controversial among career experts—the objective. Many argue against using an objective on your resume because it can hurt your chances by being either too specific or too general. Some experts tout a "skills profile" instead of an objective, while others recommend using a slightly different resume for every potential job, altering the objective to fit the specifics of the position. To avoid creating a separate resume for every job, you can

instead discuss your objective in your cover letter. Even if you choose to use an objective on your resume, you can expand upon it in your cover letter.

- A cover letter can be a window into your personality that makes the employer feel that he or she simply must get to know you better. Job-seekers who present themselves as interesting individuals are the ones employers want to interview. It's a simple concept—if you write a dull letter, they'll think you're dull, too. Given a choice between interviewing a lackluster candidate and one whose sparkling personality spills off the page, you can guess who the employer will call. Read more about how to open a window into your personality on page 23.

- The cover letter lets you impress the employer with your knowledge about the company and/or its industry. If you've done your homework, you're more likely to be invited for an interview. You'll learn more about this concept in "Demonstrating Knowledge of the Company and Industry," page 64.

- Take a look through the employment ads targeted at college grads (often labeled "professional" in newspaper want-ad sections), and count how many ask for "excellent written and verbal communication skills." Once you realize how important it is for job applicants to communicate well, you'll know what a fabulous opportunity writing a cover letter is. It's your chance to show how well you express yourself. Many job-seekers, especially new graduates, agonize over writing cover letters, but for those who understand the power of the written word, the job is easier because of the fruits it bears. If you think of a cover letter as an opportunity instead of an obligation, you're well on your way to securing many interviews.

- Finally, the cover letter is useful for job seekers who don't want to create different resumes for every opening. While you may want to create two or three different versions of your resume, you can avoid reinventing your resume for every job by using your letter to frame your qualifications in different ways.

When should you send a cover letter? Anytime you send out your resume. Never send your resume out without a cover letter. Even when employers don't specifically ask for a cover letter in their ads, they expect one. The one exception is the occasional ad that states "resumes only." That's usually a tip-off that the company is expecting many responses and plans to screen them in some way. These days, some large firms electronically scan resumes, so that a computer screens out resumes that don't contain the exact specifications the employer seeks. If you make the cut, the employer may then ask you to send a cover letter. See page 37 for more information about scanning.

Using the Cover Letter to Differentiate Yourself from More Experienced Job-Seekers

Now that you know what a big job the cover letter has to do, you may be wondering how your cover letter can compete with the letters of more experienced job-seekers. While some ads that use the words "entry level" tend to attract only new graduates, the vast majority of open positions pit new grads against candidates with a few years of experience under their belts. While that may sound like a losing proposition, it isn't. The best thing a new grad has to offer is freshness and enthusiasm. Employers like new grads because they are not set in their ways or jaded by their years in the workforce; they can be molded to fit the corporate culture. Expressing in your cover letter your desire to work with the team and fit in with the company therefore can be valuable.

Employers also like the fact that new graduates have cutting-edge, up-to-date training in their disciplines, which is especially desirable in technological fields. Thus, you may want to emphasize the quality and recent nature of your education. And frankly, employers like to hire new graduates because they are often cheaper to hire. You certainly won't want to talk about working cheap in your cover letter, but remembering what a bargain you are can help you project a positive, confident attitude in your cover letters.

Two techniques that can help you differentiate yourself from more experienced job-seekers are the Unique Selling Proposition (USP) and the PEP (Profitability, Efficiency, Productivity) formula.

Your Unique Selling Proposition

If you've ever taken an advertising or marketing class, you know that "Unique Selling Proposition," or USP, refers to the one thing about a product that makes it different from all others. In the same way, you should always try to express the one thing that makes you more qualified for this job than anyone else. Is it something distinctive about your education? Is it the fact that you worked your way through school, gaining more experience than most new grads? Is it your passion for the field? Is it that you've wanted a job like this since childhood? Your USP should answer the employer's question "Why should I hire this person?" You may not always be successful in identifying a USP, but you should always try.

Here are some excerpts from cover letters that effectively express USPs. The writer in this example seeks an entry-level accounting position:

> I have a goal-oriented personality and have proven my leadership ability and dedication to excellence. For example, as a senior in high school, I was invited to dance in the St. Patrick's Day Parade in Dublin, Ireland. To make the trip possible, I solicited funds from local businesses. I then organized and taught a dance class for children to raise the remaining money. As a result, I was able to tour Ireland for ten days, dance in the parade, and perform at the Lord Mayor's Ball in Dublin. The skills and personal qualities I demonstrated will make me a valuable asset to your organization.

The position this student seeks requires extensive computer skills:

> With a rigorous education and previous programming experience, I have much to offer Desko. The fact that I maintained a 3.5 GPA while working full-time and carrying a heavy courseload demonstrates my commitment to excellence. I would like the opportunity to continue this commitment in a position at Desko.

This student is applying for a management-trainee position:

> I am a serious, goal-oriented individual with the knowledge and power to succeed in the future. With the exception of money received through an athletic scholarship, I am fully funding my college education. My independence and responsibility have given me a higher level of maturity than many of my peers, and this maturity differentiates me from other applicants.

The next writer seeks an analyst position in the health-care field:

> A while ago, my boss told my co-workers that I did not know my limitations. He spoke the truth. I do not know the word "can't," and therefore I believe anything is possible. With this philosophy, I have gained the experience necessary to contribute enormously to your organization as a business analyst.

The management major who wrote the next excerpt is looking for a position in human resources:

> I will graduate in July 1998 after only three years in college. I have worked all the way through school in various jobs while maintaining a GPA above 3.75 and participating in many extracurricular activities. I will bring the same tenacity and dedication to this position.

This marketing major seeks an internship in the fashion industry:

> I am not a typical new graduate. I have specialized in areas of business that will help me stimulate growth in any fashion institution, I have worked extensively in fashion tailoring, and I learned much about the fashion industry—both from the retailers' and wholesalers' points of view—from my internship with the FloridaMart.

This next student seeks an accounting position:

> My internship with a local CPA firm has provided me with the skills necessary for working in an accounting firm. I am already fully trained in making general-ledger entries, completing bank reconciliations, and handling payroll data and forms. In addition, I have a working knowledge of tax preparation, estate planning, and depreciation.

The following writer is applying for a position in a high-tech firm:

> At school, I manage a difficult schedule which includes a full courseload, work, and varsity athletics. My ability to juggle these responsibilities makes me the ideal candidate for a job that requires attentiveness, teamwork, and rigorous time management.

This letter writer wants a career selling office equipment:

> I am extremely knowledgeable about your company. Because my father has worked in the copier and office-equipment business for more than thirty-five years, I have absorbed tremendous knowledge of the field by working in his office during all the summers of my young adulthood.

This student wants to apply her language skills in a customer-service position:

> I am fluent in both English and Spanish. With the growing Hispanic population in the area, my bilingual skills will significantly benefit your company.

The writer of this excerpt seeks a position in international trade:

> I am fluent in French and have a strong working knowledge of Spanish. My experience in translating texts, my work with international companies, and my knowledge of European cultures uniquely qualify me for the position at International Planning Co.

The student whose letter is excerpted next applied for an internship with a psychologist who works with hospitalized children. She described how her personal experience uniquely qualified her for the internship:

In the recent past, I have spent many long hours at the bedsides of my two brothers, who were both hospitalized for lengthy periods for separate traumas. I thus have personal experience with both short- and long-term patients and the problems they endure in the hospital.

Nontraditional students can use the USP to distinguish themselves not only from other job-seekers, but from their fellow new graduates:

I seek an opportunity to bring my skills to a public accounting firm and am especially interested in joining your team. My work experience and responsibilities for the last eleven years separate me from traditional new graduates. Working with and supervising other employees has enabled me to develop the skills needed to work in public accounting.

The PEP Formula

The PEP formula (Profitability, Efficiency, Productivity) can help you see from the employer's point of view. You should always place yourself in the mindset of the employer as you draft your letters. Think about what's really important—from the employer's point of view. They are not particularly interested in your professional development or the fulfillment of your career aspirations. Most employers want workers who can improve the company's profitability, efficiency, and productivity, so you should be prepared to say how you can do so, or how you've done so for previous employers. An employer can scarcely resist a candidate who talks about making money for the employer, saving the company money, or making the firm more productive.

Here are excerpts from letters that make good use of the PEP formula:

My primary concern is keeping corporate property expenditures down while achieving the highest possible sale price.

I monitor utility payments to ensure that our corporate clients are not paying more than necessary for required services.

My solid educational background, coupled with my diverse leadership skills, can only profit your company.

I am very excited about a career in money management, and I would greatly appreciate the chance to help you make money for your

clients. As an intern, I created spreadsheets that aided in the detection of duplicate checks paid; I saved the company almost $50,000.

My management background, military experience, and business finance education will contribute significantly to your goal of providing value-added service to your customers. I am a profit-oriented, productive individual who realizes the importance of accurate information that is provided quickly. I will provide this distinction to the sales, marketing, technical, customer-service, and credit departments, which will then render a proficient service to your value-added resellers and system integrators.

Maintaining a database can be very expensive, and outsourcing this task can sometimes be more efficient. I am confident that I can help increase the company's productivity by creating more efficient ways to maintain the databases.

I designed, manufactured and sold T-shirts during homecoming at my college. I more than tripled my initial investment in profits and set up a business that was organized efficiently. I also was a sales representative for Macy's, where I was a perennial leader in weekly sales. When it comes down to it, I can sell anything!

Quantify and Exemplify

You can also distinguish your cover letter from those of other job-seekers by quantifying and giving examples that prove the claims you make in your letter. "Quantifying" means using numbers to make your case, as in these examples:

Each summer I worked at Mayfair, I increased my sales by 50 percent over the previous year.

My weekly totals of meal sales were 20 percent higher than those of the other servers in the restaurant.

I supervised four other camp counselors.

I served a customer base of 150, the largest on my customer-service team.

A variation on quantifying is giving superlatives and "firsts":

> I was editor of the campus newspaper with the largest circulation in the South.

> ————————

> I was the first student from my school to win the coveted Parkington Chemistry Medal.

> ————————

> My supervisors said I was the most efficient and productive intern the firm had ever employed.

"Exemplifying" means providing examples that lend credibility to your qualifications, such as:

> I demonstrated my ability to work well under pressure and solve problems when a hurricane struck my hometown. I organized volunteer efforts at a local shelter and figured out an efficient way to distribute clothing to the newly homeless.

> ————————

> In my summer job at Connor Consulting, I proved myself as a team player. For example, when the mainframe computer crashed last summer, and we lost months of crucial data, I was able to motivate my group to pull extra shifts to duplicate the work.

The Three Types of Cover Letters

Most cover letters fall into one of three categories:

- The Uninvited or Cold-Contact Cover Letter
- The Invited Cover Letter
- The Referral Letter

The Uninvited or Cold-Contact Cover Letter is the most common type, since at least 80 percent (some experts say as many as 95 percent) of all jobs are on the "closed" market. Most job openings are not advertised, and employers aren't expecting to receive your cover letter and resume. New college graduates frequently send out mass mailings of cold-contact cover letters as they approach graduation, gathering large lists (sometimes hundreds) of employers in their field and mailing the same letter to all of them. Many career experts advise

against mass mailings, noting that, as with most direct-mail ventures, the response rate is only between 1 and 2 percent. They point to hapless job-seekers who spend thousands of dollars sending hundreds of letters, but who receive only a handful of interviews and no job offers.

A mass mailing, however, can be an effective tool for uncovering hidden jobs where supposedly no openings exist—as long as some simple rules are followed. Following up on your mass-mailed letter is crucial. If you don't follow up, you can expect just about the same results as if you threw reams of paper, boxes of envelopes, and rolls of stamps into the nearest dumpster. Yes, it can be time-consuming to follow up on, say, 300 letters. But if you make up your mind to make, for example, fifteen follow-up calls a day for twenty days, you can manage it. Also crucial is winnowing down your prospects list so that it is not too massive. Research the companies and choose the ones most likely to hire you.

Finally, use a mass mailing as only one part of your total job search. Responding to ads, networking, and consulting with your campus career-services office are other important parts of your job search.

Here are some guidelines and techniques for cold-contact cover letters:

- Do not send the same letter to everyone on the list. In my early, naive job-hunting days, I once sent a hundred or so identical photocopied letters to companies in a city to which I was planning to relocate. I couldn't understand why I didn't receive a response. I didn't because I had done nothing to tailor the letters to the individual companies.

- Individualize your letters by sending each one to a specific person. Not "To Whom It May Concern," not "Dear Sir or Madam," not "To the Prospective Employer." Find out who the decision-maker is in each company, and use mail-merge capabilities of your word-processing program to ensure that each letter is addressed to a person's name. (See more about this concept on page 11.)

- If possible, use the mail-merge feature or the copy-and-paste function of your computer to insert an individualized paragraph into each mass-mailed cover letter. This practice demonstrates your knowledge of each company.

- Consider using the USP technique, PEP formula, and one or more of the techniques described on pages 41 through 79.

- Make sure that your letter has a proactive final paragraph that asks for an interview (see "Closing the Sale with a Proactive Final Paragraph," page 60), and be sure you follow up. The success of your mass mailing depends on how you follow up.

The Invited Cover Letter is one written in response to an advertised opening, whether in a newspaper, trade publication, on the Internet, or the company's bulletin board. The primary advantage of the invited cover letter is that the employer wants and welcomes it, but the new graduate should take care not to be too dependent on want ads, since, as we have seen, few vacancies are advertised.

The new grad should, however, maximize every opportunity to respond to an ad by writing a cover letter so dynamic that an interview is practically guaranteed. How? By following these guidelines:

- An invited cover letter must be specifically tailored to the ad to which it responds. See "Tailoring Your Letter to a Want Ad," page 68.

- Like the cold-contact letter, the invited cover letter should be addressed to a named individual, even though the names of hiring managers are rarely included in want ads.

How to find out to whom to write the letter? Call up and ask. Letters addressed to job titles ("Dear Personnel Director") are poorly received, but even more disdained are those old chestnuts "Dear Sir or Madam" and "To Whom It May Concern." The message of the last one is that you could not be bothered to find out whom your letter concerned. The ideal person to whom to address your letter is the person with the hiring power for the specific position you seek. The second-best choice is the president of the company or another high-level executive who oversees your area. This high-level executive will likely pass your letter on to someone else, but the someone else will give your letter more attention because the honcho executive asked that the letter be handled. The last choice is the personnel or human-resources department. That department is not the best destination for your letter because its job is to *screen applicants out.* So try to get the name of the hiring manager for your ideal position, but if you can't, obtain the name of someone else with hiring power.

The only situation in which you will not be able to find out the name of the person to whom to write is when the ad is a "blind box" ad. All kinds of employers—large and small, well-known and obscure—rent blind boxes at newspapers so that respondents to the ad will not know which company placed the ad. An employer may place a blind box ad for one of a number of reasons. Sometimes employers are trying to test the loyalty of their own employees. Employers, especially those that are large and well-known, often expect an onslaught of responses to their ad and don't want to take the time and expense to acknowledge each one—but they know it's bad public relations if they appear rude by not acknowledging the responses. If the respondents don't know which company is advertising, they also won't know which employer has been so discourteous as to not respond. An employer may also place a blind box ad because it intends to fire a current employee, and management doesn't want the employee to know until a new person is in place. Finally, a company, especially a small one with limited staff, may place a blind box ad since they don't have the personnel to handle all the calls that they'd receive. You'll often see the words "no phone calls" in an ad, but some job-seekers ignore those words and

call anyway. That's not possible with a blind box ad. If you respond to a blind box ad, you can address your letter in one of three ways:

— "Dear Hiring Manager for [name of advertised position]"

— "Dear Boxholder" or "Dear Friends"

— Simply leave off the salutation and begin with the body of the letter

You'll probably come across blind box ads every time you scan your newspaper's employment ads. If an average scan yields half a dozen ads for jobs for which you'd like to apply, one or two of them will likely be blind ads. A word to the wise: Blind box ads are rarely fruitful, mostly because the job-seeker has no opportunity to follow up. In my own experience, I cannot remember a blind ad I answered that ever got a response from an employer. However, new grads who want to leave no stone unturned in their searches may wish to respond to them.

The Referral Cover Letter is an extremely effective type of cover letter that springs from networking. In it, you use a name-dropping tactic as early as possible to attract the reader's attention and prompt an interview. "Networking Your Way to Irresistible Cover Letters," page 73, explains how to use referral letters effectively.

Cover Letter Structure

You needn't follow a hard-and-fast structure in your cover letters. There is no set number of paragraphs, although your letter should be as concise as possible and certainly should not be long and rambling. Some people find writing easier when they have a structure to follow; the structure below is presented for those people. While the body of the letter is open to wide variations, the first and last paragraphs should endeavor to meet this structure's guidelines.

First Paragraph: "Why I'm Writing," or Introduction of Self and Statement of Interest. Explain why you are writing in a way that will arouse the employer's interest, specifying the type of position you seek and what you can offer. (See more about arresting opening paragraphs in "Crafting Enticing Openers," page 54, and how to use a referral in your opening in "Networking Your Way to Irresistible Cover Letters," page 73.)

The following are examples of less-than-wonderful cover-letter openings. They're weak because they make the recipient read between the lines to figure out that the writer is applying for a job. Consider how much better these

would be if the writers were more explicit about why they're writing and what position they seek!

 While I was visiting Oregon last year, the name of your station came up repeatedly in discussion as having a compelling newscast. Given my interest in broadcasting as a career, I have taken the liberty of enclosing my resume.

 There are no substitutes for drive, motivation, and desire. In December of 1997, I will graduate from Boston University with a degree in investment finance. Along with my receptive mind and the above-mentioned characteristics, I offer you a unique opportunity of propelling your already successful organization in the investments field.

My experience working as an attractions host at the Disney-MGM Studios has enabled me to understand the philosophies and daily activities at the Walt Disney World resort. I was a part of the opening crew of the Twilight Zone Tower of Terror and Sunset Boulevard. Because it was a new attraction, we had to make important decisions on our own as to how to best operate the attraction. I have demonstrated that I can work well with others by my experience in the Walt Disney College Program.

Second Paragraph—"How I'm Qualified." Briefly describe your academic and professional qualifications. Chapters of this book that can give you ideas for your second paragraph include: "Making the Most of Your College Experience" (page 42), "Emphasizing Your Transferable and Applicable Skills" (page 48), and "Accentuating the Positive" (page 57).

Third Paragraph—"Why I'm Right for <u>This</u> Job." Relate yourself to the company, giving details about why you should be considered for the job. This is a good place to demonstrate your knowledge of the company or industry (see page 64). You can also use the tools described in these chapters: "Your Unique Selling Proposition" (page 4), "The PEP Formula" (page 7), "Emphasizing What You Can Do for the Employer" (page 61), and "Tailoring Your Letter to a Want Ad" (page 68).

Fourth (or last) Paragraph—"What Steps I'll Take to Make Sure We Talk Further about My Qualifications." Request action. Ask for an interview. Tell the employer you will make contact within a specific period of time (such as a week, ten days, or two weeks). Then be sure to carry out the follow-up action you said you would. It's also a good idea in the final paragraph to tell the employer how to reach you during business hours. Even if your daytime phone

number appears on your letterhead or in the address block atop the letter, it can't hurt to repeat that contact information in the last paragraph. And be sure to mention the best way to reach you. If people can most easily reach you though e-mail, a beeper number, or a separate voicemail line, provide that information in your last paragraph.

The Closing. You can't go wrong if you use a standard business letter closing such as "Sincerely," "Sincerely yours," "Yours truly," or "Very truly yours" to lead into your signature at the end of your letter. Surprisingly, "Very truly yours" and "Yours truly" are considered more formal than the variations of "Sincerely." For a warm, friendly touch, especially if you are already acquainted with the recipient or know that the company is very informal, try "Cordially," "Best regards," "Kindest regards," "Warmest regards," or "Enthusiastically."

The Three Most Common Cover Letter Mistakes . . . and How to Avoid Them

Want to know three surefire ways to propel your cover letter into the employer's trash can? Here are the three cover-letter poison pills:

 1. Not addressing your letter to a named individual. We've seen how important it is to address each cover letter to a named individual. Your guiding principle should be that whenever it is possible to find out the name of the individual with hiring power, that's to whom you should address your letter. The only time it is acceptable to address your letter to a title is when there is absolutely no way to find out the name of the person with hiring power for that job.

 2. Failing to request an interview. As we've already noted, you need to close the sale by asking for an interview. Don't leave the ball in the employer's court. You will be far more likely to schedule an interview if you:

- take the initiative in your letter to ask for the interview,
- tell the employer in the letter that you will follow up, and
- actually do follow up.

Some employers make it a practice never to contact applicants who send them letters. They want to see which ones are assertive enough to follow up. Sometimes, especially in cold-contact letters, using the word "meeting" instead of "interview" can be more inviting. "Closing the Sale with a Proactive Final Paragraph," p. 60, shows some excellent letters that lose all their momentum by failing to end proactively. Here are some variations on effectively proactive closers for your cover letter:

> I am convinced it would be worthwhile for us to meet. I will contact you next week to schedule a meeting. Should you have questions in the meantime, please feel free to contact me at 813-555-9293. Thank you for your consideration.

> I am confident that we would find it mutually beneficial to discuss my qualifications face-to-face, and I will call at the end of next week to arrange an appointment. You are also welcome to contact me at 212-555-8283. I very much appreciate your consideration.

> I would very much like to meet with you, not only to discuss my qualifications, but also to share my graphic design samples with you. I will contact you at the end of next week to arrange a meeting.

> I would like to meet with you so that I can more fully demonstrate how well my qualifications align with the requirements of this position. I will be in Dallas in early September and will contact you before I arrive in town to see if we can arrange to meet. Please phone or e-mail me at the numbers above if you have questions. Thank you for considering me.

> I'm sure you agree that this letter and resume can't make my case as comprehensively as I could in person. I would very much like the opportunity to review with you how well I fit with this position. I know you will be recruiting on my campus next month, and I'd like to make sure I'm one of the students you interview. I will call your office before your recruiting trip here to confirm that I'm on your schedule. Thank you for your attention.

> I would like to meet with you to further explore the contribution I could make at Pennyback Systems. I will call you in ten days to confirm that you've received this package, answer any questions, and see if we can arrange a meeting or phone interview. I invite you to call me at 315-555-9293 if you need more information, and I thank you most kindly for your consideration.

> I am convinced that an exchange of information would be of mutual interest and benefit. Please review my background and

allow me the opportunity to prove that I have the credentials and capacity to make important contributions to your company. You have my commitment that your time will be well spent.

 3. Telling what the company can do for you rather than what you can do for the company. A very common error among new graduates is to see the employer as a Fairy Godparent who will wave a magic wand and help you meet your aspirations, fulfill your goals, and make your dreams come true. Remember what we said about the PEP formula: the employer wants workers who can solve problems, make money, and be productive. Making you happy is fairly far down on the list of the employer's priorities. You should always focus on telling the employer how you can contribute to the organization's success.

Here are some excerpts from letters that make the mistake of focusing on what the employer can do for the job-seeker:

 When I researched the top advertising companies in Denver, Commercial Specialists, Inc., emerged as having an excellent training program. In short, you provide the kind of professional environment I seek.

In exploring an avenue toward my career goal that would allow me to keep my current interests, I decided that real estate would best fit my personality.

I am interested in summer employment because I think it is important to supplement my academic studies through experiences in the food industry.

Note that the next example is from a letter seeking an internship. Since employers who offer internships expect interns to be major beneficiaries of the internship experience, telling what the employer can do for you in an internship letter, such as the inferior one excerpted below, is not quite as egregious as when you are applying for a "real" job. The focus of an internship letter, however, still should be on what you can contribute in the internship instead of how the internship will help you:

 This internship with Glaxo-Wellcome will give me the pharmaceutical experience I need.

 See "Emphasizing What You Can Do for the Employer," page 61, for some terrific ways to express what you can do for the employer.

Here are some further guidelines on how to avoid writing a bad cover letter:

Don't make it boring and formulaic—especially the first paragraph. If your letter is dull and uninteresting, the employer can lose interest even before he or she is finished reading the letter. The more boring your letter is, the less motivation the employer has to give you an interview. See "How to Make the Employer Sit Up and Take Notice," page 20, and "Crafting Enticing Openers," page 54, for ways to write an interesting, attention-getting cover letter.

 Don't make it too long, or with extremely long paragraphs. Your letter should always appear reader-friendly. Only under the rarest of circumstances should your letter be longer than a page. Nothing turns an employer off faster than staring at a full page of type unbroken by white space. Tread the fine line between too skimpy and nicely concise, keeping the paragraphs short and readable, limited to three sentences each. Eliminate excess verbiage; "Sharpening Your Focus," page 77, shows you how to address the most crucial points, while "How to Make the Employer Sit Up and Take Notice," page 20, offers formats that heighten readability.

 Don't ask for an entry-level job. In most cases, employers don't think in terms of entry-level jobs. They think in terms of people who have the right set of qualifications to do a certain job. Stating that you are looking for an entry-level job makes you seem like an unambitious person who views the job market from your perspective instead of the employer's. It's perfectly fine to pursue entry-level jobs, and chances are that an entry-level job is what you will obtain; just don't ask for one in your letter.

 Don't mention salary. Never include any information about salary in your cover letter unless it has been requested. Even when it is requested, you must respond to the request very carefully, as detailed in "What To Include—and What Not To," page 30.

 Don't include negative information. A cover letter should never include negative information. If there is something unusual about your situation—a skeleton in your closet, perhaps—or you lack a qualification the employer requests, rest assured that the deficiency will probably come up in the interview. That's when you should be prepared to explain yourself—not in the cover letter. New graduates are especially guilty of the bad habit of admitting they don't quite have the required experience, as in this example:

While I may not have the technical know-how that Arthur Andersen seeks in its recruits, I learn new material very quickly.

Don't fall into this trap. Do the best job you can of describing your experience, and let the employer judge for himself or herself. You may just find that your new-grad enthusiasm and your refreshing way of expressing yourself make up for any lack of experience.

See "Accentuating the Positive," page 57, to read more examples of negative traps new grads fall into and ways to avoid being negative.

 Don't sound too desperate and willing to do anything. Back when I was in college, I used to think employers would love my willingness to do anything—even pushing a broom—to get my foot in the door. This letter-writer thought the same way:

Cary Gluckstein suggested I contact you about my filling any possible openings you might have in your company.

It's wrong. Employers want workers—especially college graduates—who think highly enough of themselves that they seek jobs at appropriate levels. Employers also are not mind readers. If you tell an employer you will do anything, the employer won't know what to do with you. See "Accentuating the Positive," page 57, for more details.

 Don't display ignorance about the company to which you're writing. It's not terrible if you don't take advantage of the opportunity to showcase knowledge of a company in your cover letter. What's terrible is a blatant demonstration of ignorance, as in this example:

If your store sells tennis equipment, I urge you to consider someone like me—a tennis buff with excellent sales skills.

You should know before you ever write to a company whether it's in a line of business that aligns with your skills and interests.

Another way to betray your ignorance of the company is to spell its name incorrectly. As business majors, many of my students apply for jobs at Andersen Consulting. A surprising number misspell it "Anderson." Another commonly misspelled company name is Procter and Gamble. It's not "Proctor"!

Don't use a sexist salutation. I still occasionally encounter students who seem not to have noticed that women have fully taken their places in the work force. I still see students addressing their cover letters to "Dear Sirs" or "Gentlemen." It's just plain dumb to ignore half the workforce, and it's guaranteed to alienate any female hiring manager.

 **Don't rehash your resume.** Your letter should spotlight the more relevant parts of your resume, and it should certainly entice the reader to read it, but you should not rewrite your resume in your cover letter.

Nor should you rely on your resume to do all the work for you. Students sometimes write skimpy cover letters that say little more than: "My resume demonstrates that I am qualified for this position." If that were all there was to writing cover letters, there would be little point in the exercise.

Don't start every sentence or every paragraph with "I." Imagine how much more interesting the following letter would have been if the writer had used more variety in sentence structure and hadn't started so many sentences with "I":

> I have been referred to you by Samantha Willamette, whom you interviewed last month for a tour-guide position. She informed me that Languages Unlimited is currently searching for someone in the translation department.
>
> I am fluent in Spanish and Russian. I feel that my bilingual and international experiences will benefit your company.
>
> I am currently a junior at Ball State University, where I am working on a degree in corporate finance and a minor in Spanish. My university schedule permits me to work flexible hours in a part-time position.
>
> I would really enjoy meeting with you at your convenience and will contact your office within the next week.

See how repetitious and boring it sounds? Here's a way to fix it:

> Samantha Willamette, whom you interviewed last month for a tour-guide position, informed me that Languages Unlimited is currently searching for someone in the translation department, so I am writing to tell you how my bilingual skills and international experiences can benefit your company in a part-time position.
>
> Fluent in Spanish and Russian, I am currently a junior at Ball State University, where I am working on a degree in corporate finance with a minor in Spanish.
>
> I would really enjoy meeting with you at your convenience and will contact your office within the next week.

How to Make the Employer Sit Up and Take Notice

If one word could sum up what will make an employer notice your cover letter and decide to contact you, the word would be "interesting." If you write a letter that's exciting and intriguing, and doesn't sound like dozens of other cover letters, the employer is much more likely to call you. You can craft arresting cover letters by using the right words and reader-friendly formatting. First, let's look at some attention-getting formats.

Attention-Getting Formats

A great way to attract attention to your letter and make it reader-friendly at the same time is to use bullets. Note in the following example that the writer has framed his Unique Selling Proposition in a way that stands out and is easy to read:

> What makes me different from other applicants?
>
> - I am a skilled problem-solver with proven leadership qualities.
> - I have a special talent for establishing excellent rapport with clients, fellow employees, and students.
> - I work well under pressure while meeting strict deadlines and paying close attention to detail.

Note how effective the bulleted paragraph is in this excellent letter:

> My strong computer skills and my educational background in accounting match extremely well with the requirements for the staff accountant job your corporation has posted on the Internet.
>
> When I came across this ad I knew that I was the accountant for the job. I will receive a Bachelor of Business Administration degree in accounting from Catholic University in May 1998. Throughout my academic career, I have concentrated on accounting. I took my first accounting course my junior year in high school, and it has been my chosen field ever since. I would now like to apply my abilities as a professional in this field.
>
> I have gained experience working for Bozeman Accounting Service as a bookkeeper. The skills I have developed during the last three summers of employment with Bozeman include:
>
> - an understanding of payroll and sales tax computation
> - the ability to prepare schedules needed for client tax returns

- working skills in using Microsoft Word and Excel
- the ability to reconcile client bank statements

I am confident that my experience in and enthusiasm for quality financial accounting would be a profitable addition to your organization. I will contact you in ten days to arrange an interview. Should you require any additional information, I can be contacted at 202-555-6685. Thank you for your time and consideration.

Keywords, particularly from a want ad, can function the same way as bullets to create a reader-friendly, attention-getting cover letter, as in this example:

What makes a successful business consultant? You've listed many of the qualities in your ad for consultants at Arthur Andersen. As a new business graduate, I offer exactly the qualities you seek:

Quantitative Skills: Business consultants deal with numbers daily. Having completed a minor in quantitative methods with a GPA of 3.7, there are very few types of data that I haven't analyzed or forecast.

Communication Skills: I am an extrovert who loves to work with people. I have held executive positions in virtually every campus organization with which I affiliated myself, and every position required the ability to communicate effectively. I will use those same skills when advising clients.

Teamwork Skills: I have participated in countless group projects during my business training, and my ability to function as both a team player and a leader resulted in top grades for every group I belonged to. I also exhibited teamwork skills while participating in several intramural sports.

Another standout format, especially effective for tailoring your letter to the requirements stated in a want ad, lists the job's requirements in one column and your qualifications that meet those requirements in the second column, as seen in these two examples:

While my enclosed resume provides a general outline of my work history, my problem-solving abilities, and my achievements, I have also listed your current specific requirements for the mechanical engineer position and my applicable skills.

Your Requirements:	My Skills:
1. B.S. Mechanical Engineering	1. B.S. Mechanical Engineering
2. Engineering internship	2. Six-month internship in a professional engineering firm
3. ANSI 31.3	3. Experienced in ANSI
4. CAD experience	4. Several courses and practical experience in CAD

Thank you for taking the time to review my cover letter and resume. I am confident you will find me qualified for the position. I will call the week of April 20 to set up an interview.

Should you have any questions before then, please do not hesitate to contact me at my home number, listed above.

Your advertisement in the *Sacramento Bee* caught my eye because my experience so closely matches your requirements.

Your Requirements:	My Qualifications:
A/P and A/R experience	I receive and process bills daily in my work-study position at Fresno Pacific College's post office.
Invoicing	Prepared numerous invoices daily during summer job at Mr. Movie.
Payroll	Assisted in payroll preparation for Mr. Movie employees.
Windows 95, Lotus 1-2-3, Microsoft Word	Proficient in all three programs. I use each program daily.
Detail-Oriented	Working in a post office demands careful details and multiple tasks constantly.

As you can see, I am fully qualified to fill your advertised accounting job. I will call you next week to set up an interview. Thank you for your time and consideration.

TIP: Another great attention-getting idea comes from Brian Krueger, author of *College Grad Job Hunter* (Milwaukee, WI: Quantum Leap Press, 1997), who suggests adding a postscript, especially one that's handwritten, to your cover letter. The postscript should restate your Unique Selling Proposition in a new way. "I guarantee it will be the first thing read on your cover letter," Krueger writes. Here are some sample USPs that could be used as postscripts:

P.S. My fluency in several Slavic languages is just what Darwin needs as the firm opens new overseas markets.

P.S. I have a solid grasp of the HTML programming language, which will enable me to develop Web sites to market your company's services.

Opening a Window into Your Personality

Try to make your letter so compelling that the employer feels he or she simply must get to know you better. If you were an employer reading this poignant paragraph in a cover letter, wouldn't you want to interview the writer?

> I can make a valuable contribution to the Baptist Medical Center, especially the Fox Children's Hospital, based on my past experiences. As a child I spent a lot of time in hospitals, and I vividly remember my feelings and responses to the environment I was in. I would like to be involved in making sure that children feel as comfortable as possible in an otherwise scary situation.

Here are two more engaging letters that draw on childhood experience in a different way—by describing their early interest in the field the writers seek to enter.

> One of my most profound memories as a young child was the day I first flew in an airplane. I was traveling with my family to California, and I still remember the feeling of excitement as I held my mother's hand and climbed the stairs into the immense red, white, and blue plane. That was my first of many flights on Delta, and I have never forgotten it. I am interested in fostering that same excitement in others by working for Delta as a training instructor.

> My deep-rooted passion for travel abroad will enable me to serve your company well as an international consultant. I must confess that I have always had a passion for international travel and a curiosity for investigating other cultures. When I was a child, my grandparents filled my stamp collection with brightly colored stamps, souvenirs from their travels. I remember being so captivated by my treasure chest of stamps that I vowed to visit these places one day. I was twelve during my first overseas adventure, and since then I have pursued several adventures abroad, including extended trips to Japan, the United Kingdom and Europe, and a three-month internship with a consulting company in Portugal.

Of course, you may be able to find other ways to open a window into your personality. You might draw on humor, parental influence on your career choice, or profound life experiences, as in this example:

> While working on a summer internship with the Red Cross in Rwanda, I was exposed to human suffering far worse than anything I ever could have imagined. The misery of the people there

inspired me to dedicate my career to easing the suffering of others. That is why I am writing to you about the social-work position you currently have available.

The Academic Frame of Reference: Don't Let It Overwhelm Your Letter

Given that school has been the center of your existence for some fifteen or sixteen years by the time of your college graduation, it's only natural that you'd focus on your academic life in your cover letters. You might be inclined to list the academic honors you've received, state your GPA, list the relevant courses you've taken, and note your extracurricular activities. All of these elements of your college experience may have a place in your cover letter, especially if you have little or no work experience outside college. But when you do have appropriate experience, such as internships and co-op work, your academic experience should take a back seat. Even when it's in your best interest to emphasize your academic background, you need to describe it in a way that highlights the transferable and applicable skills you acquired in your academic training and explains how those skills relate to the job in question. "Making the Most of Your College Experience," page 42, and "Emphasizing Your Transferable Work Experience and Skills," page 48, tell you more about how to present your college work in terms of transferable and applicable skills.

Effectively organizing your letter often helps put your academic background in the right perspective. If you've had excellent career-related experience, such as an internship, information about it belongs higher up in the letter than academic details. But if your college experience is more relevant to the job you're seeking than your work experience is, emphasize your academic background first.

Note in this example how the writer focuses only on her academic experience, doing almost nothing to relate it to the job she seeks:

 I am writing to apply for the position of assistant acquisitions editor at Vintage Books that you recently advertised in the *New York Times*. I graduated from Smith College with a master's degree in humanities last May. I did my undergraduate work at Columbia, with dual Bachelor of Arts degrees in English and art history. Since receiving my master's degree, I have taken additional coursework at New York University.

In all institutions, my grade-point average has never dipped below 3.75, and I graduated *summa cum laude* from Columbia.

You will note that while attending Smith, I was selected to participate in the Semester in Florence, Italy, program. I attended classes at the Uffizi Gallery daily, absorbing lectures by some of Europe's most illustrious humanities scholars. Furthermore, while attending Columbia, I was selected to join the Humanities Society, as well as the Omicron Delta Kappa honor society.

In addition, my two years as editor of the Columbia yearbook have given me the ability to write and edit well, and my experience on the campus Publications Board has provided leadership abilities and interpersonal skills. Similarly, while attending St. Mary's Hall High School, I sang with the Madrigal Singers and helped organize a student art exhibition. I was also selected as school reporter, and I provided news about my high school to local newspapers.

The writer of the next example actually is not a very new graduate—he's been out of school for four years—but his letter shows how the academic frame of reference can weaken your letter even several years later. This job-seeker told me that in all the time he'd been out of school, he had landed only three interviews. Although the academic focus is not the only problem with his letter, you can see in the rewritten version how the letter is strengthened by subordinating his collegiate experience:

[*original version*]

I am writing in regard to the position of Recreation Supervisor, which I understand is now available.

I have recently completed my undergraduate curriculum at University of Central Florida, where I majored in parks and recreation management. During that time, I was fortunate enough to have been exposed to many different areas of recreation administration, both inside and outside of the classroom. Although I consider this past coursework influential in shaping my beliefs and attitudes regarding recreation and the people it serves, I believe it is my volunteer assignments and work experience since graduation that have given me a sound understanding of the many important concepts involved with recreation programming and administration. These past experiences have not only supplied me with a great deal of knowledge, but also given me the self-confidence to apply this knowledge as a future recreation professional.

Since leaving UCF, I have been involved in high school coaching and have been fortunate enough to have worked at a

well-known summer camp for boys, where I was actively involved in all areas of planning and implementation of activities throughout the camp. This practical experience, coupled with my strong interpersonal skills, will allow me to move on to a higher level of recreation administration in the future.

The combination of prior work experience and education I spoke of earlier has not only enabled me to acquire a good deal of experience over the last several years, but has also solidified my belief that working in a directorial capacity within the field of recreation is ultimately what I long to do.

Thank you for your time, and I look forward to hearing from you.

The letter rewritten with the academic focus subordinated:

My teamwork abilities, thorough comprehension of supervision concepts, and solid experience in developing programs will enable me to make a meaningful contribution in the Recreation Supervisor position you are currently advertising.

My experience in high school coaching has fostered the supervision skills I gained in college. I also was actively involved in all areas of planning and implementation of program activities at a well-known summer camp for boys, experiences that have honed my strong interpersonal skills. My volunteer work in recreation has enhanced my understanding of the many important concepts involved with recreation programming and administration.

My degree from the University of Central Florida in parks and recreation management encompassed a comprehensive curriculum in recreation administration. There, I developed a customer-service attitude about recreation and the people it serves, and that attitude has continued to guide my work in the field.

I am convinced of my ability to serve in a directorial capacity in the recreation field, and I would like to meet with you to discuss my ideas and philosophies. I will give you a call in ten days to see if we can arrange an appointment.

Thank you for your consideration. I look forward to meeting with you soon.

What to Include— and What Not To

The issue of the academic frame of reference brings up the question of just what should be included in the cover letter. Here's a guideline for what to include and what not to:

Always include:

- A salutation to a named individual.

- An attention-getting opening paragraph that tells why you're writing and what position you seek, and gives a pithy statement of your qualifications. It's often effective to take a risk with your opening, but be sure you don't go overboard. See "Crafting Enticing Openers," page 54, for suggestions.

- The name of your college and degree, especially if the position specifically requires a degree.

- Comments that focus on what you can do for the employer.

- Supporting material about your qualifications for the position. This material should be very specifically tailored to the position, and to keywords mentioned in the ad or job description, if applicable. It may be framed in terms of one or more of the many techniques described in this book: your Unique Selling Proposition (USP) (page 4), the PEP formula (Profitability, Efficiency, Productivity) (page 7), an attention-getting format (page 20), a window into your personality (page 23), your collegiate experience effectively exploited (page 42), and/or an emphasis on transferable and applicable skills (page 48).

- A proactive final paragraph that closes the sale by asking for an interview and leaves the ball in your court instead of the employer's.

- A phone number (as well as beeper, voicemail, or e-mail if applicable) where you can be reached during business hours. Include the phone number in your final paragraph even if it appears on your letterhead or resume. Since some employers prefer to reach you at home after hours, it never hurts to include your home phone number in this paragraph as well.

- A thank you to the employer for considering you.

- Your bold, confident signature! Blue and black ink are the safe choices; any other color is probably too flamboyant except for the most creative fields. A felt-tip pen will lend boldness to your signature, but stick to ball-point if you're unaccustomed to felt-tip.

Consider including under certain circumstances:

- Your GPA. Include it if it is exceptional or achieved under difficult circumstances (such as if you worked full-time while attending school). Resume experts say to include your GPA on your resume if it's above 3.0, so if it's at that level, you'll have it on your resume anyway and probably don't need to include it in your cover letter. Career experts debate the importance of grades in the job market; some say they are extremely important; others say employers don't care much about your grades. (My observation is that grades are more important to some employers than to others, so it's good to find out how important they are to the employer you seek to join. Your university's career services office is a good place to find out.) If you find out an employer is a stickler for good grades and you have them, you can't lose by mentioning your GPA in your letter. I have observed that, after a period of relative unimportance, grades are becoming important again in the job search. If you still have time to improve your GPA, go for it.

- Transcripts—only if requested. If your grades are terrible, you may want to skirt this request. State that you will send your transcript under separate cover or bring it to an interview, then write a cover letter so irresistible that the employer will overlook the lack of transcript—at least until you are in the interview and have a chance to explain yourself.

- A discussion of relevant courses. Include them if:
  — the employer requires certain coursework
  — your coursework was unusual. (For example, accounting majors nationwide take pretty much the same courses, so there's little reason to list your courses if you're an accounting major seeking an accounting job. But if you had a minor that adds something relevant to your coursework, or if you designed your own major, your preparation may be worth mentioning.)
  — you have no work experience and you can describe your courses in terms of the transferable and applicable skills they taught you

- Information about your extracurricular activities. As you'll see in "Making the Most of Your College Experience," page 42, and "Emphasizing Your Transferable Work Experience and Skill," page 48, activities can be extremely important. You'll especially want to discuss them if you've held leadership positions, if you can describe the activities in terms of applicable and transferable skills, or if you have little or no work experience. If you've done several internships or have other good work experience, you can give less emphasis to the extracurriculars.

- Your graduation date. If you are sending out cover letters before graduation, you should include your graduation date and your date of availability for work. If you've already graduated, use the word "recently," especially as more time passes.

- Information that demonstrates your knowledge of the company and/or industry. By all means, show them what you know—unless it makes your letter too lengthy or prevents you from discussing your qualifications.

- The name of a mutual acquaintance who referred you to the company, if available.

- Writing samples if requested, or if you write extremely well and feel that written communication is one of the most important skills needed for the job. If writing samples aren't requested but seem desirable, you can entice the employer by saying in your closing paragraph that you will bring samples to the interview.

Never include:

- Typos, misspellings, grammatical errors, or sloppiness!

- A sexist salutation

- Negative information

- All the same information that's on your resume. Highlight and call attention to your resume, but don't rehash it.

- Clichés, such as "Enclosed please find my resume" and "I have taken the liberty of enclosing my resume." The employer can see that your resume is enclosed. Don't waste words making such obvious statements.

- References. Never send references unless they are requested, and even when requested, don't include them in your cover letter or resume. List them on a separate piece of paper.

- Unsolicited letters of recommendation. These letters tend to lack credibility because no one who would write a letter for you would say anything negative about you. Sometimes the employer will ask for such letters, in which case you should, of course, send them.

- Discussion of what the employer can do for you

- Extraneous, irrelevant, or personal information

- Unsolicited salary information. Never, never, never talk about salary in a cover letter unless the information is solicited. Even then, try to avoid including the information.

More about revealing salary requirements in a cover letter. You will sometimes encounter ads that ask you to send your salary requirement or salary history. The employer is trying to find out if the company can afford you or, conversely, if your current salary indicates you're a much lower-level employee than the company plans to hire. In the case of the salary history, the prospective employer is trying to determine how often the candidate has been promoted, to what levels, and how much of a raise accompanied each promotion.

If salary is the most important issue to you, you may feel comfortable complying with requests for salary requirements or histories. After all, if the company is not willing to pay you what you feel you are worth, you probably wouldn't be happy working there. The only snag is that you could sell yourself short. The company could have been willing to pay more than your stated requirement.

When asked to supply salary requirement or history, you can:

1. Ignore the request, which is obviously risky.

2. Acknowledge the request but say you are uncomfortable discussing salary in a cover letter and would prefer to do so in a face-to-face meeting. Assure the employer that salary will not be a problem.

3. Acknowledge the request and say your salary requirement is negotiable.

Research shows that most candidates who choose options 1, 2, or 3 do not automatically get screened out—even if the ad states that candidates who fail to provide salary information won't be considered. If your qualifications are a good fit and you write a good cover letter, most employers won't put you in the reject pile because you ignored the salary request.

4. Provide your salary request BUT only after you have done enough research to know what you are worth in the marketplace. Give a very broad range and make sure you will be more than comfortable with the salary at the bottom end of the range.

To find out what you are worth in the marketplace, consult professional associations and journals in your field, people you know in your field, and the *Occupational Outlook Handbook*, which is available in most libraries. Popular periodicals frequently publish salary information; for example, *Working Woman* magazine runs a salary survey every January.

If you are willing to shell out a significant chunk of change (about $95), you can obtain accurate information on competitive salaries in your field by calling Pinpoint Salary Service at 773-4-S-A-L-A-R-Y (773-472-5279). For that price, Pinpoint will provide comprehensive salary research on one position and send you a copy of Jack Chapman's book *How to Make $1,000-a-Minute: Negotiating Your Salaries and Raises*. This book is an excellent resource and is also available without the salary service.

TIP: How do you find out what you're worth in the marketplace? Check out these sites on the Internet:

http://jobsmart.org/tools/salary/sal-prof.htm
A collection of salary surveys in various fields that
includes links to general and new graduate salary surveys.

http://204.203.220.1/cgi-bin/salary.cgi
Salary searchable database that enables you to
look up the maximum salary for a given job.

Writing and Editing with Finesse

Once you've nailed down the content of your cover letter, your next step is to write it in the most effective way possible. Everything you learned in your college composition classes applies to cover letters. Once you've developed a draft, edit it ruthlessly. A few simple tips can help you polish your draft into an excellent direct-mail piece that markets one of your favorite products—you!

- No typos or misspellings! Use your word processor's spell-checker, but also remember that the spell-checker won't detect words that are homonyms, or real words other than the ones you wanted to use (such as *form* versus *from*).

- Cut every extraneous word and all wordy phrases, such as "in order to" and "for the purpose of."

- Wherever possible, cut long, complex sentences into shorter ones.

- Let your paragraphs breathe by keeping them short.

- Check your sentence structure; transform confusion and complexity into coherence and clarity. A good way to check for awkward sentence structure is to read your letter aloud.

- Read your letter from the point of view of the employer. How would you react to this letter if you were hiring?

- If time allows, put your letter down for a day or more and see how it reads when you pick it up again. Once more, read from the employer's perspective.

- Ask other people to read it. Ask one person to check for grammar, spelling, style, and syntax, and another to check for flow and readability. Ask yet another to read it from an employer's perspective.

- Use the active rather than the passive voice. A passive verb is a verb phrase consisting of a form of the verb "to be" followed by a past participle. The subject of an active verb acts, while the subject of a passive verb is acted upon.

> **Passive:** My engineering background was used to effectively communicate our requirements to suppliers and to understand the development engineer's specifications.

> **Active:** I used my engineering background to effectively communicate our requirements to suppliers and to understand the development engineer's specifications.

A verb is passive if you can tack a prepositional phrase beginning with "by" to the end of the verb phrase: "My engineering background was used [by me] to communicate effectively our requirements to suppliers and to understand the development engineer's specifications." Check for actual or potential "by" phrases as you read over your letter. One of the most effective features of the grammar-checkers on most word-processing software is their ability to spot passive constructions.

- Use strong, vivid, active verbs. Avoid the verbs "to be," "to do," or "to work"; use more descriptive verbs.

Nondescriptive verb	Descriptive verbs
I was an accounting assistant in my most recent internship.	I provided accounting assistance in my most recent internship. I served as an accounting assistant in my most recent internship.
I did consumer surveys during my summer employment with a marketing research firm.	I conducted consumer surveys during my summer employment with a marketing research firm.
I worked in magazine advertising sales over Christmas break.	I sold magazine advertising over Christmas break.

- Watch out for apostrophe and possessive problems. My students are frequently tripped up by these little devils. To show ownership or possession, you need an apostrophe: *your firm's training program, the company's policies,*

my former employer's evaluations of me. Avoid unnecessary or misplaced apostrophes. Some writers are tempted to add an apostrophe and *s* to form a plural when they really just need to add an *s* (or *es, ies,* etc.).

Standard Business Letter Format

As a college student, you may not have a lot of experience writing business letters. While the sample letters and excerpts in this book are in acceptable business letter format, a few adjustments have been made to save space. You can use an indented-paragraph (semi-block) style, as shown in this book, or a block style with a line of space between paragraphs (not shown except in the sample that follows). This book also shows only one line (two returns) of space for your signature, while three lines (four returns) should be allowed. The book shows a standard heading with your name, return address and phone, the date two lines below, and the name of the recipient, company name, and address two lines below that. If you are pressed for space, you can leave your name out of your address block since it will also appear in the signature block. You can also place the entire return address block under your typed name at the bottom.

Although this book does not use courtesy titles (Mr., Ms.) with names in the recipient address block, such use is perfectly acceptable (and, of course, you must use the title in your salutation unless you are on a first-name basis with the recipient). The use of position titles also is optional, although it is helpful to use them, especially when you are writing to large companies. Using titles may help route your letter to the right person, but leaving them off is okay if you're trying to save space.

Keep in mind that some variations in standard format are possible. One of the most effective variations is to create a letterhead for yourself, preferably one consistent in style with your resume. Keep the design simple and conservative. Don't use ornate typefaces or cartoons, icons, or artwork.

Here is a sample of standard business letter format, followed by the same letter shown on a letterhead:

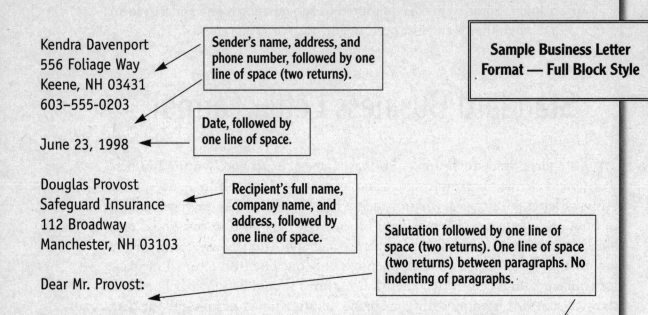

Kendra Davenport
556 Foliage Way
Keene, NH 03431
603–555-0203

Sender's name, address, and phone number, followed by one line of space (two returns).

Sample Business Letter Format — Full Block Style

June 23, 1998

Date, followed by one line of space.

Douglas Provost
Safeguard Insurance
112 Broadway
Manchester, NH 03103

Recipient's full name, company name, and address, followed by one line of space.

Dear Mr. Provost:

Salutation followed by one line of space (two returns). One line of space (two returns) between paragraphs. No indenting of paragraphs.

Dr. Gene Bartholomew of Keene State College suggested I contact you regarding a position in the Insurance Trainee Program of Safeguard Insurance Company.

During my college career, I gained considerable practical experience in sales and marketing that will enable me to make a significant contribution as a trainee with Safeguard. I also participated in a number of university-sponsored marketing research projects.

I am a May 1998 graduate whose academic record and roster of extracurricular activities attest to my worth ethic, leadership abilities, and interpersonal skills. I'm a hard worker, and I want to work hard at making money for Safeguard. As Dr. Bartholomew can attest, my education and practical experience, coupled with my maturity and marketing skills, will be an asset to your firm. I am enthusiastic about a career in insurance and am willing to relocate for your training program.

Because I am convinced of the value that I can bring to your firm, I will follow up with a phone call to see if we might arrange an interview. You may also reach me during business hours at 603–555-0203.

Thank you for your consideration.

One line of space (two returns) before closing.

Sincerely,

Allow three lines of space for signature.

Kendra Davenport

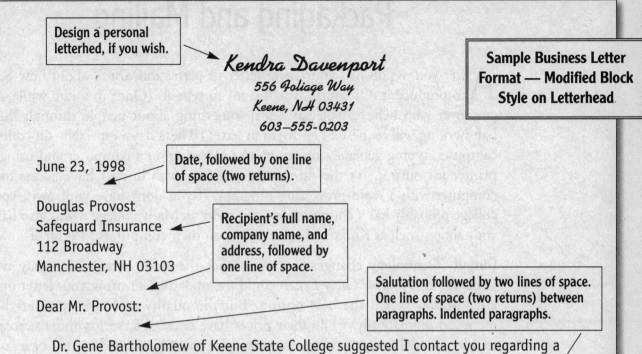

Design a personal
letterhed, if you wish.

Kendra Davenport
556 Foliage Way
Keene, NH 03431
603–555-0203

Sample Business Letter
Format — Modified Block
Style on Letterhead.

June 23, 1998

Date, followed by one line
of space (two returns).

Douglas Provost
Safeguard Insurance
112 Broadway
Manchester, NH 03103

Recipient's full name,
company name, and
address, followed by
one line of space.

Dear Mr. Provost:

Salutation followed by two lines of space.
One line of space (two returns) between
paragraphs. Indented paragraphs.

   Dr. Gene Bartholomew of Keene State College suggested I contact you regarding a
position in the Insurance Trainee Program of Safeguard Insurance Company.

   During my college career, I gained considerable practical experience in sales and marketing that will enable me to make a significant contribution as a trainee with Safeguard.
I also participated in a number of university-sponsored marketing research projects.

   I am a May 1998 graduate whose academic record and roster of extracurricular
activities attest to my worth ethic, leadership abilities, and interpersonal skills.
I'm a hard worker, and I want to work hard at making money for Safeguard. As
Dr. Bartholomew can attest, my education and practical experience, coupled with my
maturity and marketing skills, will be an asset to your firm. I am enthusiastic about
a career in insurance and willing to relocate for your training program.

   Because I am convinced of the value that I can bring to your firm, I will follow up
with a phone call to see if we might arrange an interview. You may also reach me
during business hours at 603–555-0203.

   Thank you for your consideration.

One line of space between
paragraphs and one line
of space before closing.

Sincerely,

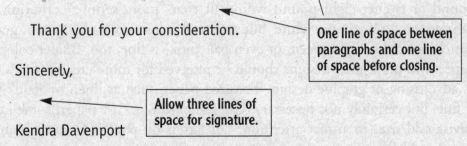

Allow three lines of
space for signature.

Kendra Davenport

Packaging and Mailing

After you've polished your cover letter to perfection, think about how best to produce it. Of course, you'll want to type it. (Once in a rare while, an employer who believes you can learn something about people through their handwriting will request a handwritten letter.) These days, especially on college campuses, typing generally means word processing on a computer and using a printer for output. It's the rare college student who doesn't have access to a computer with a word-processing program. If you don't have your own, your college probably has a computer lab you can use. Many college towns also have copy shops, such as Kinko's, that rent time on their computers to students.

Output. Technology changes so rapidly that the recommendations only two years old in *Dynamic Cover Letters* could use updating. Printing your letter on a laser printer is still the best option. But the quality of ink-jet printers has increased dramatically, while their prices have decreased, so if you have access to a late-model ink-jet printer, its output is probably as good as that of a laser printer. Just keep in mind that the ink printed by an ink-jet takes a few seconds to dry, so it can smear if you touch the surface too soon. It will also smear or blur if you spill liquid on it, but presumably you wouldn't send a cover letter you had spilled anything on anyway. Output from older ink-jet printers is less acceptable, and the output of a now-old-fashioned dot-matrix printer is definitely unacceptable.

Font. The typeface you use on your cover letter is a matter of personal taste, as long as it's not ornate, wild, or difficult to read. It's essential that your cover letter font matches your resume font. Some popular fonts for resumes and cover letters include New Century Schoolbook, Bookman, Palatino, Arial, Helvetica, and Times Roman. A point size no smaller than 10 point is suggested; 11 point is ideal.

Paper. It's best if your cover-letter paper matches your resume paper, and studies have shown that the heavier your resume paper is, the more seriously the employer will take you. Twenty-pound white bond is fine, but twenty-four-pound or twenty-eight-pound would fit that "more serious" criterion. You can't go wrong if you use white, but a neutral color (ivory, cream, tan, gray) or pastel (light blue, light green, or even pale pink) is fine, too. Bolder colors and paper with preprinted designs should be reserved for more creative fields, such as advertising or graphic design. Textured paper, such as linen or "laid" finish is fine, but certainly not necessary. Use standard 8½ x 11 paper; some experts advise odd sizes to attract attention, but letters on paper of nonstandard size are more likely to annoy than attract an employer. Don't use any kind of social stationery.

Faxing. An increasing number of employers are asking applicants to fax cover letters and resumes. For best results, make sure your cover letter is on white paper and that the black type is clearly readable (use a fresh cartridge in your laser or ink-jet printer). Small or ornate type may be difficult to read when faxed. Cover sheets are often sent with faxes, and you can create your own with contact information and spaces to fill in about the destination of your fax and how many pages the recipient can expect. You can also find a much smaller, stick-on version of a cover sheet in office supply stores. It's a good idea to mail a "hard copy" of your cover letter and resume after faxing, but sometimes only a fax number is provided in the ad.

Scanning. Many employers who screen resumes through electronic scanning do not scan cover letters; however, some do. In her book *Electronic Resume Revolution*, career columnist Joyce Lain Kennedy explains why cover letters can be especially valuable in the scanning process. Scanning systems generally include a mechanism for coding the sources of resumes, Kennedy explains. In other words, did the resume come to the company in response to an ad? Was the job-seeker referred to the company by an individual? Resumes whose sources are known and can be coded into the system often receive more attention than those whose sources cannot be determined.

If you know that a company plans to scan your resume, you should provide both a traditional and a scannable version of your resume and cover letter. Place a sticky note on the documents labeling the scannable versions for the employer's reference. How do you determine whether a company scans job-search materials? You can call and ask.

Like a faxable version, a scannable cover letter should be on plain white paper, clearly printed in black, and should not be folded. The type should contain no formatting, such as bold, italics, and bullets, nor multiple columns. Both your resume and cover letter should be produced in sans serif type. Sans serif type is unembellished, with no little flourishes on the letters:

This is serif type.

This is sans serif type.

A note about the content of a scannable cover letter: You should use keywords from the ad or job description to which you are responding. The scanner will qualify you for the job based on how well you fit the description, which in turn is based on the number of keywords in your documents that match the keywords in the job description. While virtually every book about cover letters and resumes stresses action verbs, the keywords picked up in the scanning process are almost always nouns. Specific names of software programs (Word, WordPerfect, Excel, PowerPoint) and general categories of computer skills (word processing, spreadsheet, database, desktop publishing, programming) are the kinds of nouns that scanning programs look for. The buzzwords and jargon used in the field and type of position you're pursuing are also important.

(Examples: TQM, HTML, object-oriented programming, ISO 9000, CAD, managed care).

E-mail. You will have increasing opportunities to e-mail your letter and resume to employers. See more about cover letters on the Internet in Part Four.

Regular mail. Mailing your cover letter and resume remains the most common way to get them to the employer. Many resume experts recommend sending your resume and cover letter flat instead of folded, since flat documents will sit neatly on the employer's desk, and since scanning is always a possibility. If you mail your documents flat, you will need a large envelope, ideally 9 x 12, which also works well if you include enclosures such as transcripts, writing samples, or references.

When to mail? Since most newspaper want ads are printed on Sunday, the greatest number of responses to those ads arrives on Tuesday. Also consider that Monday is the heaviest mail day in a typical office—your package may get more attention if it arrives on a day other than Monday or Tuesday.

Delivery services. Overnight delivery is an option if you need to get your cover letter to another city quickly. Overnight packaging also can make an impression on the prospective employer, although the chances that the hiring manager will see your package are somewhat slim; usually a secretary or clerk opens the mail. If you need your package delivered locally and quickly, you can hire a messenger service.

Hand delivery. Delivering your cover letter and resume by hand can be highly effective because few people do it. If you're brave enough, you can camp out outside the office of the hiring manager and ask his or her assistant if you can have five minutes of the manager's time. If you're successful, you get a jump on all the other candidates, not only by handing your cover letter and resume to the hiring manager personally, but also by gaining an advance mini-interview. Even if you don't get to meet with the hiring manager, making a good impression on the manager's assistant is helpful.

Record keeping. Keep track of which employers you write to, and exactly *what* you write to each employer, since your letters will vary in their content. One way to keep track is to print out an extra copy of each letter and, where applicable, attach the ad to which it responds. That way you won't be clueless when the employer asks you over the phone or in the interview about something you said in your letter. Since your letters will be dated, you'll also have a record of when you sent each one so you know when it's time to follow up. You can keep the letters in a binder or you may want to keep your records on a spreadsheet, such as the one found on page 39, which you can photocopy. Systems using index cards or your favorite computer program also are options.

Cover Letter/Job Search Log

	Company Name	Contact Person	Phone Number	Position Applied for	Date Letter Sent	Follow-up 1	Interview	Follow-up 2	Follow-up 3
1									
2									
3									
4									
5									
6									
7									
8									
9									
10									
11									
12									
13									
14									
15									
16									
17									
18									
19									

PART TWO

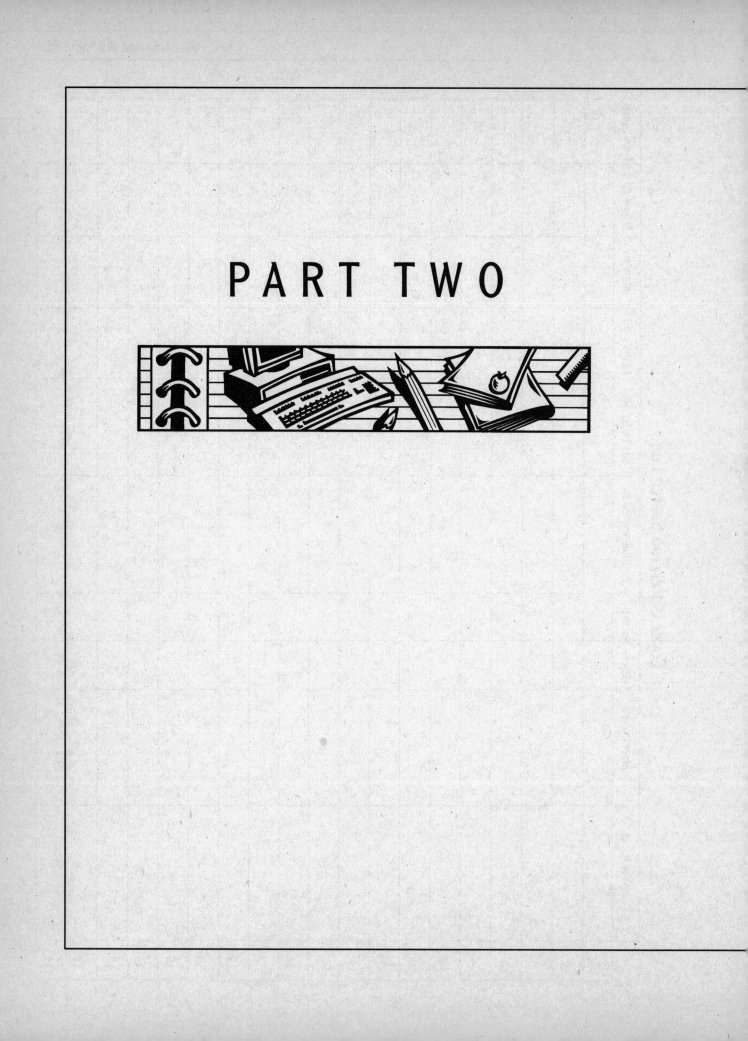

The Top Ten Ways New Grads Can Write Can't-Miss, Dynamic Cover Letters

You've mastered the prerequisites. Now it's time to advance to upper-level cover-letter writing. Here's the real nitty-gritty, the techniques that will make your cover letter stand out from the crowd. You'll discover that being a new entrant into the workforce can be an advantage instead of a liability.

Making the Most of Your College Experience

More and more college students are realizing that a successful balance of academic study, extracurricular activities, and work experience gained in internships and summer jobs paves the magic road to that post-graduation job. But what if your experience is not so well-rounded? What if you have little or no work experience? What if you realized too late that you really should have been more involved in extracurriculars, done an internship, or worked in (or even outside of) your chosen discipline during your breaks from school? You can still maximize your college experience.

Think about all of your college experience, including classes and extracurricular activities. Consider first your classes. Many students undertake activities in classes that provide experience that's as valid as that gained in paid jobs. Such activities include class projects, research papers and projects, group projects, hands-on assignments and "real-world" experiences, laboratory experience, presentations, study-abroad programs, and simulations.

Look, for example, at your school's special programs and the hands-on projects you've done in classes. Stetson University, where I teach, has an unusual program in the finance department in which students invest real money in a stock portfolio. Such a program provides an excellent way to make the most of your college experience in your cover letter, as in this example:

> For the past year, I have been part of the Roland George Investment Program, the only undergraduate program in the southeastern United States that allows students to invest real money in the stock and bond markets. The program has allowed me to gain practical experience in portfolio management and has enhanced my communication and teamwork skills. I have also fine-tuned my research techniques in order to make the best stock and bond selections.

In other classes at my university, students create World Wide Web pages and work with real clients to critique and improve their pages. Marketing students conduct research for actual clients as well. I've seen students successfully construct entire resumes based solely on the experiences they've gained in their classes, and the same can certainly be done with cover letters.

Thus, ask yourself about all your academic accomplishments:

- Did you write a software program, or design a Web page?
- Did you excel in any competitions?
- Did you ever achieve the highest grade, the best test score, or the strongest essay?

- Were any of your poetry, plays, stories, music, or art published, performed, or exhibited?

Next, consider your extracurricular, volunteer, and community activities:

- What leadership positions did you hold, and what skills did you demonstrate?
- Did members of your group choose you for or elect you to a position of responsibility? Did you choose to take on additional responsibility?
- What do your friends and classmates ask you for help and advice about? What are your areas of expertise?
- What community service projects did you undertake?
- Did you use organizational or managerial skills?
- How did you improve your organization?
- Did you handle money or budgets? Did you raise, collect, or manage funds?
- In what ways did you exhibit interpersonal skills?
- Did you train, teach, or orient organization members? Did you speak in public or write for an audience?
- Did you employ problem-solving, conflict-resolution, or mediation skills?
- Did you deal with the public? What skills did you use? Did you respond to complaints or smooth ruffled feathers?
- How did you demonstrate teamwork, drive, and determination (for example, as an athlete)?
- Did you have to juggle many projects simultaneously under deadline pressure?

Finally, while the responsibilities of work-study positions might not seem relevant at first, you can probably come up with at least one applicable skill if you scrutinize what you did. Reliability and a strong work ethic are among the desirable characteristics you can demonstrate.

Now let's look at some excerpts from letters in which the writers make the most of their college experiences:

> While pursuing my degree, I have worked on many group projects related to marketing. The most extensive project was a collaboration among team members to implement a marketing strategy for merchandising Guess Jeans in Spain.
>
> In addition to my challenging and competitive academic program, I have taken many courses that directly relate to consulting. In my Small Business Management class, for example, I consulted with a Nassau County law firm. The consulting work included research and presentations and focused on hardware and software selection, marketing, and reengineering.

Note that in the next example, the writer not only describes the information systems he developed as part of his coursework, but also explains how that experience can benefit the company he's writing to:

> Ted Pizzuto suggested I contact you about the accounting position available at Baldwin Corporation. He informed me that Baldwin is looking for an applicant with experience in accounting and computer information systems.
>
> As a student majoring in accounting at the University of Miami, I have gained a great deal of knowledge about accounting. I understand that Baldwin wishes to hire someone who can develop an information system to track sales and inventory. During the course of my studies, I have developed several information systems related to customer orders, using Microsoft Access, Excel, and Visual Basic.

In the next excellent excerpt, the writer effectively portrays her experience in her sorority as every bit as valid as employment experience:

> My recent experience as director of finance for an organization of sixty individuals and my classroom knowledge as an accounting major will benefit your company. I have successfully completed many assignments at my previous place of voluntary employment, Pi Beta Phi. I worked independently to reconcile bank statements and accounts receivable, bill accounts receivable, prepare accrual journal entries, generate financial statements, create an incentive program, and establish a computerized accounting system. Just as I completed these assigned goals effectively, I will be productive, proficient, and accurate for your company.

The next writer highlights both her classroom and extracurricular experiences. An accomplishment such as organizing a "Celebrity Baggers" event at a local supermarket might not sound like much, but note the kind of job this young woman seeks. She wants to be a development manager—a fund-raiser—so the ability to convince people to give their time and money is an important skill. She nicely underscores her fundraising abilities in the second paragraph:

> My internship with Blue Cross-Blue Shield has given me the opportunity to fully utilize my marketing skills in a nonprofit business organization. Most importantly I have gained greater insight into the cause of the American Lung Association. I would use the income development manager position to achieve all the goals established in the mission statement of your organization.
>
> I conducted a study on the motivational behavior of charitable donors by using my communication skills and computer programs (DataEase, Excel, PowerPoint, and several other business software

programs). I successfully filled a local grocery store with faculty members in a Celebrity Baggers fundraiser during my first month as an intern.

Finally, I have always been able to enlist the help of students and professors to partake in or donate to philanthropic events occurring on campus. My motivational skills, persistence, and creativity at work and in the community provide me with the insights needed to be a successful income development manager.

Note how this writer demonstrates his qualifications by blending his academic background with his work-study experience assisting professors:

Both my academic and employment experience have prepared me well for a career in business information systems. My training includes developing, designing, and documenting information systems and decision-support systems. I have learned various programming languages, including Visual Basic, Pascal, Personal COBOL, and Assembly.

My previous employers can affirm that they have entrusted me with major responsibilities and that I have quickly adapted to each of these positions. For example, as a teaching assistant for Lehigh's Department of Decision and Information Sciences, I manage grade analyses for three professors. I also coordinate the allocation of audiovisual and computer equipment for faculty and student use, and I am developing a decision-support system in Visual Basic to automate the process. In addition, I have designed, programmed, and implemented a management-information system that helps students target prospective employers.

This student uses a combination of examples from her work-study and extracurricular experience to broadcast her talents:

As a computer lab assistant I gained invaluable hands-on experience in computer software problem-solving and was promoted to assist professors in coordinating and implementing technical software seminars. My effective interaction with the faculty led to my receiving a very prestigious position as the co-teacher of a university class designed to orient first-year students on Auburn's campus. I took full responsibility for the theme, syllabus, class discussions, and lectures.

As the elected vice president of membership for my sorority, I planned, delegated, and coordinated the entire recruitment and selection process for new members. After demonstrating my leadership and responsibility in that position, I was elected vice president of administration.

The new grad who wrote the next letter responded to an ad that listed discretion, good organization, communication skills, and the ability to work with minimal supervision as qualifications for a human resources assistant position. Note how the writer uses his extracurricular experience to show that he meets these qualifications:

> My recent success as president of Alpha Tau Omega demonstrates my leadership ability and communication skills. As head of the organization, I have been accustomed to working with little or no supervision, and I have learned the value of confidentiality. Further, I have proven that I am a well-organized, responsible, and reliable individual who excels at working under pressure.

The following letter also makes good use of extracurricular experiences:

> While attending college, I dedicated considerable time and energy toward revitalizing AIESEC, a nonprofit international student-run business that matches highly motivated students to paid internships at international companies. Being part of AIESEC allowed me to share my passion for international travel with others. This combination of international exposure and academic achievement, as illustrated by my resume, makes me an ideal candidate for Pan-Pacific Consultants.

Seeking an internship with a radio station, the next writer draws on relevant experience on campus:

> This year, as a junior at Barnard College, I have become involved in a concert promotion project co-sponsored by our marketing and music departments. This project has given me the opportunity to work closely in various aspects of the marketing field.

The writers of these next three excerpts do a good job of connecting their extracurricular activities to specific skills that apply to the jobs they seek:

> My success as vice president of public relations for Student Ambassadors demonstrates my leadership ability and communication skills. I organize open houses for prospective students and their parents, and create and publish an information sheet about the organization and its members.

> _____

> As the coordinator of a tutoring program for disadvantaged youth, I have developed my organizational and communication skills, as well as my determination and solid work ethic. The same skills that aided me in recruiting 115 new volunteers for service projects this year will make me a valuable asset for your organization.

> _____

My experience demonstrates my motivation, leadership ability, communication skills, and ability to work well with people. I planned and organized a fundraising project that raised $10,000 for Sussex County local charities.

This writer nicely outlines applicable accomplishments in school and work:

I have spent the last four years studying business at Babson College, where I have maintained a 3.2 GPA. These years have provided me with a good business background and have sparked my interest in the underwriting and claims aspects of insurance.

I am a highly motivated self-starter. I established a house-painting business to help pay part of the cost of college, an experience that taught me to work as hard as I can to achieve my goals. As rush chairman of my fraternity, I was motivated to make my organization the best. While only eight new members were initiated the year before I took office, twenty-two new members pledged when I held the position. The national organization recognized this accomplishment when we received a special award for recruitment. This maturity and drive can similarly benefit your organization.

Although the next writer neglects to mention his academic background, he does a nice job of describing how his college baseball career and other activities have given him the skills he needs for his chosen field:

My successful background as starting pitcher for a highly competitive baseball team, along with my involvement in various team-based activities, make me an ideal candidate for a position in human-resource management.

As a third-year member of Baylor's baseball team, I have participated in various volunteer projects, such as home improvement in the community and fundraising activities for the team. I have also conducted baseball camps for local children that required leadership and training skills.

With my experience, skills, and interest in management, I would be of immediate benefit to your organization. I can bring supervisory and leadership skills to your team, having successfully motivated individuals and coordinated their activities.

Remember, you must relate your college experience to the job you seek. In the following example, the writer talks in the second paragraph about extracurricular experience that may or may not relate to the marketing job she seeks. But then in the third paragraph, she describes money-handling experience that has nothing to do with marketing. Her work as a waitress may very well relate to marketing, but she needs to frame it in a way that details that relationship:

I am in my junior year at the College of William and Mary, and I am seeking summer employment in marketing.

As an officer of the Panhellenic Council and of my sorority, I gained experience in dealing with a variety of individuals, organized informational sessions for more than one hundred students, scheduled and participated in rehearsals for skits and productions, and planned activities and criteria for pledges to meet and complete before initiation.

I also gained experience handling large amounts of money and balancing accounts as the treasurer of the Order of Omega, a leadership organization, as well as in my position as a waitress.

Be careful, too, that your attempt to maximize your college experience is not too much of a stretch, as in the case of the writer of this letter who attempted to draw a connection between the experience needed for a job in radio and all the partying he had done in college:

  I have also had the opportunity to gain some knowledge of the radio and music industry through many social engagements over the past few years.

Emphasizing Your Transferable Work Experience and Skills

The college student who has been wise enough (or broke enough) to garner some work experience while in school may hold a competitive edge over the classmate who's done little more than hit the books for four years. If the work was at the lowest level and outside your field, however, the experience can seem difficult to relate to your first post-college job. How can someone who has been a server in a restaurant every summer portray himself or herself as God's gift to marketing? How can the retail associate at the mall appear to be a fabulous teacher? How can the low-level office clerk position himself or herself as exactly the person an accounting firm needs?

It's all a question of breaking down your previous jobs, no matter how lowly they seem, into the transferable skills they provided you with.

Let's first look at the overarching skills and qualities emphasized by career experts. Patrick O'Brien, in his book *Making College Count*, lists Seven Winning Characteristics every employer is looking for. In his *College Grad Job Hunter*, Brian Krueger enumerates Ten Critical Success Factors. Donald Asher presents a Profile of an Ideal Candidate in his *From College to Career*. Certain characteristics are common to all three lists:

- Oral and written communication skills

- Teamwork and interpersonal skills

- Leadership skills

- Work-ethic traits, such as drive, stamina, diligence, ambition, initiative, reliability, and positive attitude toward work

- Logic, intelligence, and proficiency in field of study

These five skill clusters can be considered the most important in your first post-college job, and some or all of them will be required in just about any job in your career. You can hardly go wrong if you describe in your cover letter how your previous experience has provided you with one or more of these skills.

Let's break these skill clusters down further to reveal more transferable, applicable skills that you can cite in cover letters.

Communication Skills

- Speaking effectively, giving presentations
- Listening
- Writing and editing
- Expressing ideas
- Interviewing
- Reporting information
- Facilitating group discussion
- Providing feedback
- Negotiating
- Persuading

Teamwork and Interpersonal Skills

- Creating an environment that fosters productivity
- Establishing good working relationships
- Supporting others
- Perceiving feelings, situations
- Counseling
- Motivating others
- Sharing credit
- Cooperating
- Delegating
- Asserting your opinions and those of your organization

Leadership Skills

- Setting standards, priorities, and goals
- Initiating new ideas
- Coordinating efforts and tasks

- Assigning responsibilities
- Managing groups
- Keeping track of details
- Managing conflict
- Weighing alternatives and making decisions with others
- Reviewing programs, including quantitative evaluation
- Measuring performance
- Coaching
- Teaching
- Selling ideas or products
- Promoting change

Work-Ethic Traits

- Being punctual
- Managing time
- Meeting goals
- Setting and meeting deadlines
- Accepting responsibility
- Enlisting help
- Attending to detail
- Organizing
- Implementing decisions

Logic, Intelligence, and Proficiency in Field of Study

- Forecasting, predicting
- Identifying problems
- Defining needs
- Developing evaluation strategies
- Gathering information
- Imagining alternatives
- Coming up with ideas
- Identifying resources
- Extracting important information
- Solving problems
- Planning and budgeting
- Setting goals

Career counselor Patrick O'Brien boils down his list of winning characteristics into just two "career commonalties," noting that "whatever a person does, his or her job is to do two things: solve problems and satisfy customers. The problems and customers can be tremendously different depending on the field, but at the end of the day, that is what a person is paid to do. On a global level, employers are looking for the same characteristics."

Beyond these commonalities and the five skill clusters, experts mention additional sought-after skills and characteristics, including:

- Entrepreneurial skills, a popular contemporary buzzword that encompasses the skills that people use when they start their own businesses. These skills include the capacity to be a self-starter, the ability to manage projects, and a talent for marketing oneself.

- Confidence

- Flexibility

- Ability to acquire new technical, analytical, computer, or foreign language skills quickly

- Ability to follow orders

Now, let's look at some lower-level jobs that college students typically hold while in school and examine how—in a single paragraph—students describe these jobs in terms of transferable, applicable skills.

Server in restaurant seeking entry-level marketing position

In addition to my marketing coursework, I have employed marketing and customer-service skills in the restaurant field. In my most recent position, I marketed appetizers, desserts, and other add-ons to customers and added value to their dining experience. I would like to apply the same sales savvy and interpersonal skills in the marketing position you have open.

Retail associate seeking teaching position

As a sales associate in a retail store, I successfully handled customers' needs every day. To succeed, I had to be a patient and diplomatic problem solver. Because the same kinds of patience and creative problem-solving are required of teachers, I am confident I will be an effective third-grade teacher at your school.

Office clerk seeking entry-level accounting position

The office clerk job I held every summer throughout college demanded a high degree of organization and detail-orientation. My experience also taught me the importance of fitting into the office culture, and I stand ready to become a contributing member of your team.

Babysitter seeking position as management trainee

As a former caregiver to three active youngsters, I know the importance of good time management. I've gained that skill, along with exemplary leadership, organizational, and communications talents that will contribute to our mutual success when I join your management trainee program.

Bank teller seeking entry-level position in a stock brokerage

I seized the opportunity in my bank teller position to learn as much as possible about personal finance and investments, while simultaneously honing the "people skills" that are crucial to success as a stockbroker.

Fitness instructor seeking entry-level position in health care

Having worked my way through college as a fitness instructor, I have already demonstrated my commitment to good health. Further, I developed the solid customer-service skills that will enable me to effectively interact with patients.

Computer-lab assistant seeking position in consulting

My work-study position as a computer-lab assistant involved solid knowledge of technology, the ability to teach that technology to fellow students, and the skills to assist students who had problems with the software and hardware. To me, that's what consulting is all about—possessing the knowledge to teach and assist clients and the interpersonal skills to do so successfully.

Resident advisor seeking sales position

I am very excited about contributing my talents in the field of professional selling. I have heard a number of times that sales skills are taught, and there is no such thing as a natural-born salesperson. I couldn't agree more! I have served as a resident advisor for two years, and I was very surprised at how much selling goes on. I have learned quickly that the more you know about your customer, your product, and how to adapt to each situation, the easier the sale becomes. My success in selling my ideas to residents and administrators makes me an ideal candidate for your training program.

Telemarketer seeking position in hotel management

My work as a telemarketer required me to communicate with a diverse array of people, some of whom represented difficult challenges. I refined my communication skills to the point where I was nearly always able to smooth ruffled feathers, solve problems, and provide satisfaction to customers. These are exactly the skills that are vital to effective hotel management, and I am eager to apply my talents at your hotel.

Here is another excerpt that effectively exploits transferable experience and skills. The writer of this example, who seeks a position with a scenic design firm, does a good job of acknowledging that the job she wants requires the ability to be a self-starter and teamwork skills, and she tells how she acquired both those characteristics:

Some art work is solo, while some projects require the efforts of many hands. I work well independently as well as in teams; my first job was as a self-employed jewelry maker and seller. As a two-sport varsity athlete, I also know what it takes to achieve team goals.

Now let's think about the transferable skills you've gained in the classroom. Here I must give a tip of the hat to Fred Jandt and Mary Nemnich for their discussion of transferable skills gained from school experiences in their book *Using the Internet and the World Wide Web in Your Job Search* (Indianapolis: JIST Works, Inc., 1997). These skills include:

- **Ability to thrive under deadline pressure.** College is a cornucopia of deadlines, so if meeting deadlines is important to the job you seek, by all means stress your ability to do so.

- **Ability to handle multiple tasks.** Remember how you wanted to smack your instructors for assigning simultaneous major papers and projects? Multitasking is increasingly valued in the workplace, and your cover letter is a chance to describe your ability to juggle many projects at once.

- **Ability to achieve goals.** Your good grades are proof of that skill, so do discuss them if they're exemplary. You may have met other goals while in school, too, such as graduating in three years instead of four (which may be why you don't have any job experience). Any goal you've met while in school is potential cover-letter fodder.

- **Ability to adapt.** Your college years probably gave you your first opportunity to make adult decisions and act independently. How did you handle stumbling blocks and disappointments along the way? The way you rose above difficulties can provide solid examples in your cover letter.

- **Writing skills.** Jobs that require good writing skills are a lot more common than you probably think. If you demonstrated your ability to write well in college, highlight that skill in your cover letter. And of course your writing talents should be evident in your cover letter as well.

- **Research skills.** How many people who've been out in the "real world" have research skills that are as fresh as yours? How many know as much as you do about conducting research on the Internet? Probably not many, so emphasize your research skills when this ability may be helpful in a position.

TIP: For specific lists of marketable skills in a wide range of majors, visit the Career Doctor at the Student Center on the World Wide Web:

http://www.studentcenter.com/cgi-bin/doctor.dll

Crafting Enticing Openers

The opening paragraph of an effective cover letter should do three things:

1. Tell why you are writing, so that the recipient doesn't have to wade into your letter to determine what it's about. Just about everyone who receives cover letters and resumes is a very busy person who wants you to get to the point as quickly as possible. It's not enough to say in the opening paragraph that you seek a position with that company; to truly get to the point, you must be specific about exactly which position you seek.

2. Convey this information in a way that grabs the reader's attention.

3. Your opener should not grab attention for the sake of grabbing attention but should give the reader a sense of what you can do. It should contain a pithy statement—which you'll elaborate on later in the letter—about how you can meet the company's needs.

Compare these two openers, for example. Both do the job of telling why the writer is writing, but which one would make you want to know the letter-writer better?

 I am writing in response to your ad in Sunday's *Sentinel* for a medical salesperson.

My training in marketing and sales in the medical industry offers much to a company that seeks motivated individuals in its sales force. I have recently graduated from Clemson University, and am eager to put my solid education to work in a position such as the one you advertised in Sunday's *Sentinel*.

Here are more attention-grabbing openers:

Having been employed with Hawaiian Tropic, I know firsthand that your corporation is a strong and growing organization in which I could meaningfully contribute the management and marketing experience I've gained through both education and experience.

 Perhaps you should not consider me for an internship unless you want an energetic, dynamic, and dedicated individual. In a fast-paced and growing world, it is important to be flexible, open-minded, and prepared for change. In addition to possessing these

attributes, I am confident that I can make a valuable contribution, using information technology and management training garnered through both education and experience.

After reading your advertisement in the newspaper, I knew I had to contact you immediately. As requested in your ad, I am a highly motivated person who will work hard for your company. I firmly believe I possess the tools to help your company thrive.

As a seasoned cruise traveler and worker in the hospitality industry, I am well aware of your company's status as an industry leader. My education and experience in marketing, customer service, sales, information systems, the Spanish language, and worldwide travel would enable me to enhance the success of Royal Caribbean Cruise Lines.

I was excited to see the position of marketing coordinator for Mamma Mia's Pizza in Sunday's *Star Ledger*. I am currently a delivery person for your Glen Ridge location and am very impressed with your company's values, philosophies, and of course . . . your pizza! My past work experience, education, and knowledge of the company would enable me to contribute to the success of Mamma Mia's Pizza.

What person interested in working in the rental car business wouldn't want to bring motivation and talent to the industry leader? I am extremely interested in working in this industry, and that's why I'm applying for the manager trainee position.

Over the last four years, I have been an avid consumer of your company's automobiles. I have a passion for what your company produces, and I know I can infuse this same energy in all the work I do for you. I have a solid educational background, as well as extensive experience in a number of related fields, and I would be thrilled to contribute my talents to your organization.

I would like to become an asset to your management staff as a general office manager. I am convinced that O'Dell & Lee, Inc. will benefit from my prior experience at your office and from my training as a management major at Arizona State University.

Since one of the main purposes of your letter is to get you an interview, a particularly arresting opener is one that asks for an interview right off the bat. Note the confident tone of this opener:

> I'd like to talk with you about becoming a management trainee with your firm. When I join your company, I will bring with me not only a strong educational background but also the dedication to get the job done.

Sometimes you have to take a risk if you want to grab attention with your opener. Do you find the following example, in which the writer uses a "stream of consciousness" approach, catchy or too risky?

> Standard and Poor's ratings . . . Consulting for pension funds . . . Stocks, bonds, and mutual funds. They are all in a day's work for a productive stockbroker.

Most of my students find that one too risky, especially since stock brokerages are conservative places. The following example is a bit risky, but less than the previous one because of the creative nature of the field:

> Call off the search; you've found what you are looking for! A fresh mind eager to become a productive part of Scenic World's creative team. I am an artistically inclined student at Emerson College, looking to combine my painting and drawing talents with making profits for a business like yours.

Similarly, the next risky opener would probably work because of the free-wheeling nature of the sport of surfing:

> Surf's up! Not only are the waves clean and glassy, but you are holding in your hands a promising resume. Look no further because I am the perfect person for your sales position.

How to test whether your opener is too risky? Since the degree of risk you can get away with is directly related to the field you seek to enter, your best bet is to show your letter to someone in that field. Be sure to sound genuine in your opening paragraph. In the next example, the writer attempts to use the referral/name-dropping approach but it comes off sounding phony, more like ad copy than something someone would actually say in conversation:

> I was commenting to Will Benner that the firm of Edwards and Caldwell is the ninth-largest firm in Central Illinois, providing high-quality accounting services for construction firms, real-estate companies, and nonprofit organizations.

Don't sound presumptuous in your opener. Many employers receiving a letter that starts the way the next example does would resent the letter-writer's telling her what her next step should be:

👎 Congratulations on your expansion into the Pittsburgh area. Now that you have attained a new market, the next crucial step is selecting the right person to run this store.

Negativity never has a place in a cover letter, but getting off on a negative foot is especially inauspicious in your opening paragraph. The opener in the following example is truly unfortunate:

👎 I apologize for missing you and Mr. Medgars on your recent visit to Rutgers University.

Accentuating the Positive

If there's one trait that sets the cover letter of a new graduate apart from that of a more experienced job-seeker, it's the lack of confidence that new grads tend to project. Because their talents are largely untested in the job market, new grads tend to sound tentative, hesitant, and even weak, wimpy, or downright negative. Here are some of the lack-of-confidence traps that new grads can fall into, and how to avoid them.

- Avoid phrases such as "I feel" and "I believe." New grads sometimes lack the confidence to make bold and self-assured statements about themselves, so they frequently qualify their statements. It's best to either leave off the qualifier or use a stronger qualifier, such as "I am confident," "I am convinced," or "I'm positive." Note how in the following examples, the writers' statements are more confident without the qualifiers.

Instead of using a weak qualifier	Use a stronger approach
I believe my background provides me with unique qualifications . . .	My background provides me with unique qualifications . . .
I feel very confident that I would be an asset . . .	I am confident that I will be an asset
I feel I can help the ABC Corporation to become more efficient . . .	I am convinced I can help the ABC Corporation to become more efficient . . .

- Value judgments are more credible if substantiated by third parties. There's nothing wrong with making value judgments about your talents and qualifications. But they'll carry more weight if you say they are substantiated by former employers or professors. (And be sure your third party will back you up on any claims you make!)

Instead of making a value judgment about yourself	Attribute to professors or former employers
I am organized and detail-oriented, as well as motivated and dependable under pressure.	My professors can attest that I am organized and detail-oriented, as well as motivated and dependable under pressure.
I can handle major responsibility and I adapt well to change.	Previous employers will affirm that they have entrusted me with major responsibility and that I adapt well to change.

- **Use active, strong verbs.** Make yourself sound active and in control. Don't make it sound as though your accomplishments in school and previous jobs just happened—show how you took an active role in making them happen.

Weak	Stronger
I received many awards for the highest sales in the store.	I earned many awards for the highest sales in the store.
In my most recent experience, I was placed in a leadership position and received honors for both academic and leadership excellence. My assigned squad leader required me to assign duties to the members of my squad and made me accountable for their actions.	In my most recent experience, I took on a leadership position and earned honors for both academic and leadership excellence. I assigned duties to the members of my squad and was accountable for their actions.

- **Concentrate on positive information.** New graduates sometimes feel they must reveal every detail about their background and even point out their weaknesses. The opening of the following example weakens the whole sentence:

 Although I have not had the opportunity to gain a wide variety of experience in finance, I have gained general experience in my field through internships and stock-trading simulations.

If you simply eliminate that negative opening clause, you strengthen the statement enormously, and you remain completely honest:

👍 I have gained general experience in my field through internships and stock-trading simulations.

- **Don't sound too desperate.** Another way new grads shoot themselves in the foot is by sounding too desperate and willing to do anything. While you might think employers appreciate flexibility from job applicants, the opposite actually is true; they much prefer applicants who know very precisely what they want to do, unlike the writer of this example:

Desperate and willing to do anything	Specific about the position sought
I would like to emphasize that I am looking for experience in the "real world" of marketing this summer. As a result, I would greatly appreciate any position that you could offer.	Because I am looking for experience in the "real world" of marketing this summer, I would greatly like to make a contribution in a marketing research internship.

- **Avoid overblown language.** Don't be so positive that it comes off sounding phony, as in this example:

👎 I am writing in response to the employment advertisement of juvenile care worker as listed in *The County Leader*. I share a deep concern for and commitment to humanity, especially our children.

After reviewing the enclosed resume, you will be convinced that interviewing me will be mutually beneficial. I am anxiously awaiting the opportunity to fulfill my responsibility to all humankind.

- **Avoid statements regarding on-the-job learning.** Employers don't like to be reminded of the time and expense required to train new employees. New grads who lack certain skills are often tempted to qualify their weaknesses by saying they are "willing to learn" or are "quick learners," but ask yourself if it is really necessary to make such a statement. If you feel you must address a weak skill, a phrase that works well is "get up to speed."

Weak	Better
Although I have not worked with Lotus spreadsheets, I am a fast and willing learner.	As for your requirement for spreadsheet experience, I've worked with Excel, a program even more advanced than Lotus. Thus, I have no doubt I can quickly get up to speed on Lotus.

Closing the Sale with a Proactive Final Paragraph

As we saw in Part One, failure to close your letter with a proactive final paragraph in which you ask for an interview and tell the employer you will call to arrange that meeting is one of the biggest mistakes cover-letter writers make. To illustrate the importance of being proactive, let's look at two truly excellent letters that fall apart because they lack a proactive closer.

My strong academic background in political science and international relations will allow me to contribute to the state and local reporting position you are currently advertising.

Municipal reporting demands the abilities to comprehend, analyze, critique, and translate complex government issues. The Stockton State political science department has transformed me into a well-informed and knowledgeable person in government affairs. The department has acknowledged my special abilities to study and communicate political issues. During my junior year I was chosen from a selected group to participate in the 25th annual Student Model Senate.

My courses also emphasized verbal communication skills, analytical, and creative writing skills. These are the skills that will enable me to effectively communicate to your readers.

I am available for an interview at your convenience. I may be reached at 609-555-3106.

Thank you for your time and consideration.

The omission of a proactive closer in the following example is even more egregious because the writer is applying for a sales position.

Are you seeking an experienced sales representative? Could you use an eager salesperson who achieved success while working in the competitive automobile industry? I am that salesperson.

Through my previous sales experience and my bachelor's degree in business administration, I am certain that I can help lead Newave Electronics into the 21st century. In addition, my willingness to learn, well-developed written and oral communication skills, and self-motivation all qualify me as a valuable team player.

I am very interested in the position available in the Seattle market area. If necessary, relocation to any other market area is not an impediment.

I believe my qualifications and your needs are an excellent fit. I look forward to your response. Thank you for your time and consideration.

This writer doesn't even *mention* an interview, let alone ask for one. If he can't close the sale for an interview in his cover letter, how can the employer expect he will close sales on the job?

Also avoid inadvertent phrases that could take you out of contention. The following phrase, which I've seen on more than one cover letter, suggests to the employer that he or she should tuck your resume away in a drawer instead of calling you for an interview:

Enclosed is an updated version of my resume for your files.

Here's a good proactive closer that attempts to seize the opportunity to interview with the employer at an upcoming conference:

My resume and cover letter can convey only a limited sense of my qualifications. I will be attending the Nikon Sales Seminar in Dallas, Texas, in June, and would like to schedule an interview then. I will contact you by May 15 to arrange a meeting either at the seminar or at another time. Should you wish to contact me before then, my number is 510-555-7345. Please leave a message if I am not available. I look forward to meeting with you. Thank you for your time and consideration.

Emphasizing What You Can Do for the Employer

We saw in Part One that talking about what the employer can do for you instead of what you can do for the employer is another major cover letter mistake. Telling how you can increase the employer's Profitability, Efficiency and Productivity (the PEP formula) is one way to convey what you can do for the employer. The key to is to take your positive qualities and qualifications one step further, not only listing those great traits, but telling the employer very specifically how those skills will meet the company's needs.

These examples paint a vivid picture of what the writer can do for the employer:

Six years of involvement in restaurant management have taught me about every facet of the industry. Through those years our family-owned-and-operated company expanded from a single unit

into a nine-restaurant chain. Having been brought up in the business, I've dealt with a diverse array of individuals. I have developed, among other attributes, strong entrepreneurial, interpersonal, and motivational skills, which will contribute to a fruitful and lucrative partnership with your company.

In addition to an undergraduate background in business and sales, I have interned with the Sheraton Great Lakes, where I was involved in selling that five-star hotel's accommodations to tourists from all over the world. Add to that experience my understanding and appreciation for the sport of golf, and you have the perfect addition to your golf-equipment sales team.

To be successful as a marketing manager, you must know what the customer wants. My four years of service in the customer-service department at Builder's Square while completing my education have provided me with valuable insights into customer needs. As a member of your marketing team, I will not only strengthen your product line, but will also contribute to the entire company's success.

Here are several more good letters:

My extensive training and hands-on experience is the perfect fit for your company's needs. I am a graduate of Slippery Rock University with a marketing degree and extensive experience in sales. I look forward to succeeding in the position as head sales manager at Telemark, Inc.

My background in sales comes from two summer internships in which I progressed from sales representative to assistant sales manager in the telemarketing department and was hired full-time the next summer as the manager. This experience, coupled with my education, is a sure-fire asset to your bottom line. My creative and aggressive nature will benefit your company significantly, and I know that I will generate the results you are looking for.

Because I recently worked in one of the convenience stores in your company's chain, I am well-acquainted with how to prioritize tasks. When I worked there last summer, I oversaw the organization of the task list that employees had to use. While corporate headquarters provided the basic structure of the task list, I modified it to meet our store's needs. This summer I would like to be able to do that for all the corporate stores.

Working in "the problem store" as you often called it, I am certainly aware of the difficulties, and, fueled by my management classes, I have some ideas about how to solve them.

Your sales representative, Bernie Donalds, suggested I contact you about the sales representative position that will soon be opening in the Bay Area. Upon my graduation in May from the University of California, Berkeley, I can make a profitable contribution to Minolta's sales team.

My academic career, work experience, and knowledge of photography have prepared me well for this position. I have studied retail sales, professional selling, and sales management through academics and work experience. I have earned several awards from Minolta for my knowledge of the equipment and for my sales performance. I am accredited to sell both Minolta's professional and amateur lines. I achieved my Professional Systems Sales Award the first year of my employment with Berkeley Camera Exchange.

From my work experience, I know the value of good employees. To succeed today, a human resources professional must excel through effective recruiting, training, and relations with employees. My bachelor's degree in human resource management can help me contribute to the Home Depot family. I would like to put my knowledge to work for you. My experience can help develop new and innovative programs to continue the company's success as the world's largest home improvement retailer.

The managerial, organizational, leadership, and communication skills I have acquired from employment and extracurricular activities will enable me to make a substantial contribution in a human resources assistant position in your corporate office.

My extensive experience with customer relations and quality customer service, accompanied by my education and management experience, would provide an outstanding and profitable asset in one of the customer service manager positions you are seeking to fill in the Glasgow and Inverness branches of your ever-expanding institution.

My education and coursework, combined with my previous customer service experience, has made me recognize the need for satisfied customers, and I am fully capable of providing satisfaction to the fullest extent.

Remember the student who wrote the creative opener in her letter to the scenic design firm? In her closer, she does a nice job of summarizing what she

can do for the company, again using language that would not work for every type of job-seeker:

> You need someone who can apply her skills and help keep Scenic City moving along steadily. I am that someone, and I will be in touch next week to set up a time for us to meet. Your artistic team is a professional palette of colorful minds; make me a new hue on your palette, and I will mix in with your colors to create a masterpiece.

Demonstrating Knowledge of the Company and Industry

One of the best things you can do—and something many job-seekers fail to do—is to show off what you know about the employer's company, or even the industry in general. It doesn't take a huge amount of research to write a few sentences in your letter about the company, and if you interview with the company, you'll want to research it before the interview anyway. Demonstrating knowledge of the company commands the employer's respect and attention because you've done your homework. Most letter-writers who demonstrate knowledge of the company also tend to flatter the employer, whether overtly or implicitly, and that flattery certainly can't hurt.

These excerpts demonstrate company knowledge and, in some cases, flatter the employer:

> I am interested in exploring the possibility of an accounting internship with your company. I chose your firm because of its excellent reputation and aggressive commitment to the accounting profession.

> For some years now, I have been an admirer of Birnbaum Investments' many subsidiaries and its ongoing quest to introduce products that capture diverse aspects of the tourist industry. Birnbaum appears to be the company for future innovation in Barbados tourism, and I know I can contribute to its continued success.
>
> Having been previously employed at Walt Disney World, I understand that customer satisfaction is the main priority in achieving success in the theme-park business.

I enjoyed your informative presentation at Bowdoin College so much that I was inspired to research PharmaCom further. In doing so, I discovered that my professional demeanor and sales talents would be an excellent match for the third-largest drug company in the world. I notice in your annual report that PharmCom streamlined its labor force in 1995 because you are committed to quality rather than quantity, a philosophy that aligns directly with my characteristics. My solid academic performance, work ethic, drive, organizational skills, and strong interest in the pharmaceutical industry should provide evidence of my ability to produce outstanding results for your company.

The writer of the next letter learned through his research that the corporate headquarters of a large hotel chain was relocating and would need a human resources representative in the new location to hire local people and ease the transition for those that would be moving with the company:

I was very excited to learn of the human resources representative position you are offering. I see this position as a great opportunity to help your company through this transitional period, and am convinced that my enthusiasm and creativity will help smooth your move. Further, my work ethic and organizational skills will mold your incentive programs into real morale-boosters at a challenging time.

Research isn't only effective for showing a prospective employer that you've done your homework; it also can be a powerful technique for uncovering hidden opportunities. Demonstrating knowledge works extremely well in cold-contact cover letters because it enables you to address the needs of the employer even when those needs have not been advertised. Annual reports, business periodicals, and the Internet are just a few excellent sources for company research. So are the people who work at the firm. Notice how the authors of these paragraphs have used such research information not only to impress prospective employers, but as a way to crack the hidden job market:

I was pleased to read in your annual report that your company has implemented a Total Quality Management program, because TQM was the focus of much of my management coursework and individual research in college. I possess the know-how to help propel your TQM program to success.

When I read in the *Wall Street Journal* that your company plans to install a companywide ZapNet network, I was excited, because I have developed expertise in ZapNet programming and

troubleshooting through my information technology studies and internships.

_____

I was delighted to learn that your company plans to make a major investment of funds and human resources in establishing a presence on the World Wide Web. My thorough knowledge of the HTML programming language, along with my exemplary performance in my Internet marketing classes, will enable me to hit the ground running on your Web marketing team.

_____

I am aware that cost-cutting will continue to be a major priority for your hospital, and I am therefore convinced that my ideas on achieving cost-effectiveness while maintaining quality patient care make me the perfect addition to your purchasing department.

_____

An article in _Business Week_ noted that your company's major thrust for the next five years will be to increase market share for the Tend-a-Pet product line. I have innovative ideas for increasing market share, and my education has equipped me to implement those ideas for you.

_____

The business press has reported that deregulation has led to ever-increasing competition in your field. I have the training and savvy to assist you in maintaining your competitive edge.

_____

I was excited to read about your new software product, GPA-Builder, a sure winner. My enthusiasm for this product, combined with my comprehensive software knowledge, ensure that I can effectively sell this program for you.

_____

The fact that your company is planning a strategic alliance with Bevco interests me greatly, not only because I've studied a great deal about effective strategic alliances, but also because I did an internship last summer at Bevco.

_____

Your annual report notes that your company's growth rate is approximately 14 percent per year. I'd like to be part of the team that keeps the firm on that upward trajectory.

_____

When I read on the Internet of your company's major plans for globalization, I couldn't wait to contact you. My fluency in three languages, study-abroad experience, and solid education in international business can only benefit you in this expansion.

———————

Learning of your company's commitment to the professional development of its employees was extremely meaningful to me because of my coursework in employee-training programs and my demonstrated presentation skills.

Since mission statements are trendy, your knowledge of the company mission statement or operating philosophy can have a strong impact:

The mission statement of the St. George Lumber Company, which I read in your annual report, is inspiring to me because I share its values of respect for the environment, dedication to customer service, and concern for shareholder profit.

In addition to specific company knowledge, awareness of trends and current events in the industry can also strengthen your cover letter:

Fortune magazine reports that the trend toward outsourcing is continuing to grow. I'm sure that means your consulting firm is eager to add well-educated, enthusiastic new faces—like mine—to its team.

———————

Emerging trade agreements between nations are bound to affect your business. I did my senior research project at Brown University on trade agreements and would like to discuss some of my ideas with you.

———————

I don't pretend to know any more than the next person about whether interest rates will rise or fall. But I began following the stock market long before I earned my degree in finance, and I know how to respond to market fluctuations and calm worried investors.

———————

Having played tennis for many years, I am aware that the equipment a tennis player uses is extremely important. Through my international and collegiate experience, I have learned a great deal about the tennis industry and how it functions. In this market-driven industry, the quality of an organization's marketing department is the basis for the firm's success. I am convinced I can provide that quality and competitive edge.

Tailoring Your Letter to a Want Ad

If you want your cover letter to stand out among the multitudes of responses the average want ad receives, you must respond to the requirements listed in the ad. Identify the keywords and buzzwords in the ad, use them in your response, and you'll sound like the answer to an employer's prayers.

By the way, new grads often miss opportunities to respond to want ads because they don't meet all the qualifications listed in the ad, but if you feel you can do the job, go ahead and respond to the ad. Most employers consider ads wish lists; they'd *like* to find someone with all those qualifications, but they might be perfectly happy with a new grad who lacks a skill or two but projects a winning attitude in the cover letter.

To see how effective it can be to tailor your response very specifically to the ad, let's look at a want ad and two responses to it. First, the ad:

PAYROLL ACCOUNTANT I

Trico Services Co., a multiplant conglomerate, has an opportunity for a payroll accountant responsible for processing corporate payroll, tax reporting, proper accounting, and continuous improvement strategies. Requires technical knowledge of both payroll processing and information systems. Four-year degree and/or three years' experience in discipline preferred.

The two letters sent in response:

#1   My strong academic background in accounting and information systems will allow me to contribute greatly to your company as a payroll accountant.

During my four years at Albright College, I concentrated my studies on accounting and information-system-based courses. I performed very well in these classes, and I feel my education has prepared me for a promising career in the financial industry. Albright has kept up with the latest technology in the business field, and this is conveyed to the student body on a continual basis in coursework. This will allow me to bring new ideas to your company.

As you can see from my resume, I am highly qualified for the position open in your financial division. . . .

#2   My education and experience in accounting, payrolls, and information systems will allow me to fit the position you are advertising. Through my education and experience in management, accounting, and the use of various information systems software packages, I can contribute significantly to Trico Services Co.

I will receive a bachelor of business administration degree in May 1998. My education is coupled with my extensive experience with the use of electronic spreadsheets in payroll accounting. I am also familiar with the use of other information systems, such as databases and word processing, in the practice of accounting and payroll processing. I can therefore contribute my abilities to accurately analyze and interpret data, as well as my attention to detail.

Now if you were the employer who had placed that ad, which respondent would you be more likely to call? The writer of letter #1 or letter #2? The first writer's initial two paragraphs are reasonably appropriate, if not as specifically targeted as they might be. The end of the second paragraph, about how his college kept up with technology, is only marginally relevant to the position and has little to do with the applicant's qualifications. The paragraph also mentions the ability to "bring new ideas to the company," but this probably is not a position in which new ideas are particularly sought. The writer then notes that his resume shows he is highly qualified for the position, but in reality, his resume did not prove him to be qualified. He might have been able to make a case for himself and overcome the weak spots in his resume in his cover letter, but he didn't.

Compare that example to letter #2, and notice how often the writer of the second letter uses the keywords "payroll accounting." This is the applicant the employer is more likely to believe is a match with the position.

Here's another good example of tailoring a cover letter to an ad. First the ad:

ADMINISTRATIVE ASSISTANT

For a young, aggressive data processing company. The individual should be extremely organized, articulate, multitasking with office management potential. Must be able to communicate effectively and possess excellent verbal and written skills. Must have PC experience with MS Windows, Word, Excel, and Money; technical writing experience helpful. Our company provides a complete benefit package and excellent growth potential. Send resumes to: Personnel, c/o TRC, 824 Benguiat Drive, East Longmeadow, MA 10572 or fax 413-555-2282.

Note how the respondent picks up on the language of the ad and makes herself sound extremely well-qualified:

A junior at Amherst College, I am majoring in investment finance. My courseload has also included several semesters of study in information technologies, so that I might stay abreast of the newest developments in the computer industry. As your ad requests, I have PC experience with MS Windows, Word, and Excel. I am organized, efficient, and possess solid communications skills.

Your ad speaks of an excellent potential for growth in the position I am applying for. If I were writing an ad to you, it would say the same. By allowing me to join your team, I am confident that our company will grow and prosper, reaching even higher realms of success.

I will call your offices soon to arrange an interview appointment.

More examples of effective tailoring:

Your ad in the *Asbury Park Press* for an accounts receivable assistant leads me to believe you seek a person with my ability to handle multiple tasks, including receiving rent payments, collecting tenants' reporting requirements, and assisting with clerical duties. Through my education and experience in accounting and the use of various information systems software packages, I can contribute significantly to Real Estate Investment Company.

I will receive a Bachelor of Business Administration degree in accounting with an information technology minor from Temple University in May 1998. I am well-accustomed to multitasking, having worked for Shop-Rite as a back-office cashier balancing receipts at the end of the night. I also collected payments of bounced checks. As student director of the Temple cafeteria, I delegated work to my student managers and front-line workers and handled the payroll for each month.

I am fluent in all the computer software packages you list in your ad—Windows 95, Visual Basic, WordPerfect, and Lotus 1-2-3.

My experience and background with international cultures coincide remarkably well with the requirements for the communication skills in the customer service position you recently advertised in the *Sacramento Bee*.

Having come from Costa Rica, a tourist-oriented and service-dedicated country, I am well prepared to meet your customers' needs. I am bilingual in English and Spanish, and I have communicated effectively while working at many bilingual restaurants and at processing plants in Costa Rica and Alaska.

The ad this student responded to asked for a manager who could thrive in a fast-paced atmosphere and possessed good communication and teamwork skills:

> I couldn't agree with you more! A planning manager must thrive in a fast-paced atmosphere. I personally love the fast-paced lifestyle. In fact, for the past two years I have maintained a 3.4 GPA while keeping actively involved in many campus activities and holding a part-time job. Obviously, I can successfully manage a fast-paced working environment.
>
> Like me, every person that applies for this position will meet the technical and distribution experience qualifications this position demands. However, I also possess all of the intangible qualifications you mention in your ad. The courses I have taken have helped me develop exceptional oral and written communication skills. As well as having these courses under my belt, I also have the advantage of being from the Charlottesville area, so I will be able to identify with your customers and establish effective communication with them.
>
> I have developed excellent teamwork skills through my work with various charities and in executive roles in many campus organizations. My leadership in these diverse groups demonstrates my passion for working with and learning from other people.

While some cover letters fail to target the ad as precisely as they might, others miss the bull's-eye by a much wider margin. One way to overshoot the mark is to portray yourself as overqualified. Normally, it's not that easy to seem overqualified, even for an entry-level position, but if you're applying for a summer job, for example, it's not unusual to get yourself screened out. A perfect case in point is the following letter written to a major theme park that advertised for seasonal part-time workers. Companies seeking seasonal part-timers usually pay these workers lower wages and offer limited, if any, benefits. They may be wary of applicants who want to use such a position as a stepping stone to a career in the company. The assumption is that someone that intent on moving up will not be content with the seasonal part-time job, and so the person is not perceived as a good fit. Don't get me wrong; it's perfectly okay to be ambitious and even to express that ambition to the employer. But the best venue for telling the employer about your desire to be promoted quickly is the interview, not the cover letter. Thus, as a response to an ad for seasonal part-timers, the letter excerpted next would have a good chance of going to the "reject" pile:

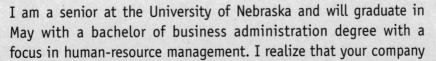 I am a senior at the University of Nebraska and will graduate in May with a bachelor of business administration degree with a focus in human-resource management. I realize that your company

promotes from within, so I wish to obtain a part-time position in hopes of advancing to a managerial position upon graduation.

Another way to miss the mark when responding to an ad is to describe qualifications that are not congruent with job requirements. The writer of the next example did a great job of using his military experience to describe some high-level responsibilities he'd held. The only problem was that he was applying for an accounting position:

> The military played a major role in my development as a team player with the discipline to succeed. Some of my responsibilities consisted of maintaining the multimillion-dollar sonar system and the fire-control system onboard the ship.

You also need the tone of your letter to match the job's requirements. The writer in the next example is applying for a public relations position at a television station. While public relations people are generally expected to be bubbly, enthusiastic, good writers, the writer of this letter has crafted a yawner. Her opener is far from a grabber, her last paragraph fails to close the sale, and her letter contains none of the pizzazz one might expect from a would-be public-relations staffer:

> I am interested in applying for a position in the public relations department of your television station. It would be an honor to work for a television station of such stature.
>
> Over the nine months that I have been interning for WEXU, I have realized that it is the most reputable public broadcasting station in the South Texas region. I have learned a lot about the public-relations field of communications, and I have benefited greatly from my experiences at WEXU. I know that if I were a part of the public relations team, we could all work together in order to continue the station's success in enriching, educating, and entertaining our community.
>
> I look forward to hearing from you soon. Thank you for your time and consideration.

Networking Your Way to Irresistible Cover Letters

A referral cover letter can be the most effective kind of letter of all, not only for the attention it commands but also because the recipient would consider it rude not to interview someone referred by a mutual acquaintance. Remember that any name you drop in a referral letter should come as early as possible to grab the recipient's attention. These three techniques will help you come up with many names to drop in your referral cover letters:

Begin networking as early as possible. Tell everyone you come into contact with what kind of job you're looking for. In all likelihood, your contacts will multiply, as one person with whom you've networked suggests someone else to talk to. Virtually anyone can be a contact: people you meet at social events, family members, professors, classmates' parents, guest speakers, or members of professional organizations in your field.

Keep a list of these contacts in an organized fashion, such as on index cards, in a notebook, or in a collection of business cards. Six months to a year before graduation, contact everyone on your list and ask them more specifically if they know who's hiring for the kind of job you want. The names they give you become automatic targets for referral cover letters.

Conduct informational interviews. Informational interviews are enormously helpful anyway, but they're also terrific for providing contacts for referral letters. These interviews can also help you clarify your career goals. I require my students to do three informational interviews during a semester-length course. They frequently discover surprising information about their chosen career fields that motivates them to shift or even completely change their goals. You can also learn a great deal about the cultures of individual companies and decide if they might be good places to work. But most significantly, informational interviews provide valuable contacts and insider information about how to get a job in a given company. In his classic job hunting guide, *What Color Is Your Parachute?* (Berkeley, CA: Ten Speed Press, updated annually), Richard Bolles offers great insights about informational interviewing, as does Patrick Combs in *Major in Success* (Berkeley, CA: Ten Speed Press, 1994).

Ideally, begin conducting informational interviews a year and a half to two years before graduation. Simply call or write someone who holds the kind of job you are interested in. (Examples of informational interview request letters are on pages 96–97.) It does not have to be someone with hiring power; in fact,

it's frequently better if it's not. Ask if you can take about thirty minutes of his or her time to learn more about the field and the job. Then compose some questions and go interview the person. At the end of the interview always ask for more suggestions of people in the field you should talk to, and either interview them too, or put them on your contact list. Six months to a year after the interview, write a letter to your contact explaining that you're now seriously in the job market and interested in interviewing with your interviewee's company.

Informational interviewing also enables you to find out more about a company's needs, so that when you do your actual job interviewing with the organization later you can focus on its needs and how you can meet them much more sharply.

TIP: There's a wealth of information about informational interviewing on the World Wide Web. Just a few of the many sites include:

What is informational interviewing?
http://www.umassd.edu/careerserv/interviewskills.html#inter

Informational interviewing
http://danenet.wicip.org/jets/jet-9407-p.html

Informational interviews
http://www.kaplan.com/career/Info_Interviews.html

Supervisors and co-workers from an internship or summer job can become targets for self-referral letters. If you performed well in your job or internship, a self-referral to one of these contacts can be really powerful, because you have already proven that you are an asset to the company.

Here are some examples of the referral and self-referral approaches:

Referrals

> My adviser, Dr. Andrew Williamson, and I have discussed how my skills might fit in with your planning for your next conference, in November 1998. He said he had discussed with you the possibility that I could assist you in the conference's preparation.

> _____

> Your colleague Jared Zarkisian suggested I send my resume directly to you. We talked about your current need to bring sales professionals in to augment Vanguard Standard's electronics marketing, and how well I could fulfill that need.

Referrals and self-referrals based on informational interviews

I'm sure you remember my informational interview with you last November. The insights you provided into fashion merchandising were invaluable to me, and I thank you again for giving so generously of your time and information. I'm now closer to graduation and would like to meet with you again to discuss the possibility of my joining your firm.

I enjoyed speaking with you at the University of Tampa Accounting Career Day, sponsored by our campus FICPA chapter. I had previously gained valuable information about your firm when I conducted an interview with Hillary Tyrrell last year. Ms. Tyrrell gave me constructive insight into exactly what is involved in this type of career, and what skills are needed. Based on what she told me, I'm convinced my skills and experience are a perfect fit.

Angie Stevens suggested I contact you about the opening you have for an assistant curator at your museum. When I interviewed Ms. Stevens about six months ago to obtain information about a career in museum work, she mentioned that the museum is looking for an efficient system for cataloguing its collections. I've given this issue some thought and would like to talk to you about how I could maximize your cataloguing efficiency in the assistant curator position.

You will recall that I interviewed you last April to collect information about the magazine publishing industry. I notice that you now have an assistant editor position open. Recalling our discussion about the difficulties of getting staff members to meet deadlines, I wondered if I could share my ideas with you while interviewing for the assistant editor position.

Referral based on networking at a professional meeting

Your colleague, Nikki Voorman, and I met a few days ago at the Big Bend Advertising Federation meeting. She informed me that you are interested in hiring a motivated individual who can sell your new line of jet-propulsion watercraft. I have the background and personality to excel in this capacity.

Self-referral based on internships and summer jobs

Thank you for the opportunity to work for you this past summer. Working with the kids was a very valuable experience, and next year will be even better. I am aware that the position will become available again at the end of 1999.

———————

My past experience as an intern in your department and my academic background in management will enable me to immediately contribute to the administrative assistant position that is open.

Self-referral based on meeting at a career fair

It was a pleasure speaking with you last week at American University's career fair. I was particularly impressed by Atlantica's philosophy and hope that you will consider my resume in your search for new consultants.

Self-referral and referral in opener

I enjoyed meeting with you at Kriner Pontiac-Buick-GMC Truck in Poughkeepsie last summer. Bill Howard, the fleet manager at Kriner, suggested I contact you regarding possible openings in the financial management department of the Fleet Division.

———————

I truly enjoyed speaking with you on the phone last week. When Dr. Garrison informed me of the upcoming internship in your promotions department, I was thrilled. My ability to communicate well and my strong interest in the music industry will enable me to make a genuine contribution to WAVE 105.9.

Self-referral based on social encounter (always be sure it's appropriate to refer to recipient by first name)

Dear Rick:

Once again, I must thank you for the interesting conversation we had at Christie's and Ken's wedding last week. I appreciated the information you gave me on the airline industry and the insights you provided about the company's work environment. I am writing in response to your invitation to share my resume with your company.

Self-referral with flattery added

> Thank you for the opportunity to have lunch with you during your visit to Azusa Pacific University. I also attended your seminar here regarding Wal-Mart and found it interesting and informative. I understand from our lunch that you are hiring college graduates in your marketing department.

Sharpening Your Focus

The need for specificity, or sharply targeting an employer's needs, has been an ongoing theme of this book. It should be obvious that your cover letter should be as precisely focused as possible. Describing your experience and your transferable skills is only the first step. To be truly effective, you must tell how your experience and skills will help the company be more profitable, efficient, or productive. Your cover letter should not rehash your resume, nor be so skimpy that it asks the resume to do all the work of selling you to the employer. Among the unfocused types of cover letters I've seen, especially ineffective are what I call "the Autobiography Letter" and the letter with "Kitchen Sink" paragraphs, in which the writer has thrown in everything but the kitchen sink. Following are examples of two types of letters you don't want to write.

The Autobiography Letter. This letter rambles on and on without focus, telling the reader of the writer's exploits, but doing little to connect those experiences with the kind of job the writer seeks:

> I am currently a senior finance student at Brandeis University in Waltham, Massachusetts. After receiving my bachelor's degree in July, I will be relocating permanently to Hungary to seek full-time employment. Recently, while researching material for a term paper, I learned of Doppler Systems' presence in Central Europe.
>
> I am very interested in working for a reputable American firm with an interest in establishing and expanding business in this area of the world. As a part of my degree requirements, I have taken courses in marketing and multinational finance and have emphasized both investments and financial corporate reporting. My minor is in the German language, and I satisfied the requirements of this study, partially, by studying one year abroad at Albert Ludwig's University in Freiburg, Germany.
>
> During my two semesters in Freiburg, I took advantage of semester breaks and vacations to travel with fellow exchange

students to their homes in Hungary. I also took introductory Hungarian while attending Albert Ludwig's University.

In addition to my scholastic pursuits in Germany, I spent three and a half years as a U.S. soldier stationed just outside of Frankfurt, and one year as a track worker for a firm under contract to the German railroad. The latter position took me to various locales throughout the country.

The combination of formal training and real-life experience has allowed me to become extremely fluent in German. My intention now is to become equally proficient in Hungarian.

The Kitchen Sink Paragraph. Note that this paragraph, the middle one in the writer's cover letter, describes at least five different skills. The writer should not only split the paragraph into two or three smaller ones, but also expand on how these skills qualify her for the job she seeks:

I also have vast knowledge of the Latin culture. Since I was born and raised in a Latin American country, it is very easy for me to relate and understand the needs of other countries. I am hard-working, independent and reliable, a combination that is not easily found in many individuals. While a member of the varsity tennis team, I demonstrated strong leadership skills that I will put to work towards the benefit of your company. My coach, Kathryn Riley, as well as many of my professors can testify this fact. I possess extensive knowledge about computers and software programs like Word, WordPerfect, Excel, Access, and others, which will allow me to deal with modern business techniques in a dynamic environment. I am detail-oriented; I could deal with much information and still find the pertinent facts of the matter.

Here's another Kitchen Sink paragraph that's too long and contains too many ideas that are not only unconnected to the job the writer seeks as a computer programmer, but also unconnected to each other. He makes a stab at telling how his degree in philosophy will help him as a programmer, but he needs to do more to justify his qualifications, with such an unrelated degree:

For nearly three years I have been a student computer technician for Academic Computing Services at Bucknell University. I am responsible for the repair and maintenance of all faculty, staff, and computer lab machines on campus. My duties also include the maintenance of our network and servers. I am also a lab supervisor for Academic Computing Services. I am also responsible for designing and maintaining several of Bucknell's home pages for the World Wide Web, experience that has provided me with a detailed knowledge of the HTML programming language. In August 1998, I will complete my bachelor's degree in philosophy. My liberal arts

background has equipped me with exemplary communication skills. I have taken several math and computer science courses in my college career. My mathematics background includes Trigonometry, Statistics, Calculus I and II, Linear Algebra, Logic, and Discrete Math. I have also taken several computer science courses. In these courses, I work with Assembly, Pascal, and C/C++. I am currently programming using C and C++ in the Windows 3.1 and Windows 95 environments.

As we've discussed, you need to be very specific about the kind of job you want (especially in the opening paragraph), and how your skills and qualifications apply. In this example, the writer is too general about what she wants to do and how she is qualified:

I am a student at Bryn Mawr College majoring in communication studies. I am interested in a position in either the broadcasting or advertising fields. I am a highly competent team member with hands-on experience in the advertising industry.

My major interests are advertising and promotions. I am extremely motivated, I work hard, and I believe that my interpersonal skills and my ability to speak four languages will complement any position that deals with both the broadcasting and advertising fields.

Another way to sharpen your focus is to give examples, as described in "Quantify and Exemplify," page 8.

PART THREE

Sample Letters for Special Situations

Internships, externships, and summer jobs are growing more and more important because employers increasingly seek graduates with some experience while in school. You will probably have the opportunity to write a cover letter in pursuit of one of these pre-graduation opportunities long before you start your post-graduation job search.

Job search correspondence doesn't stop with the cover letter. Following up is extremely important. You must thank the employer for your interview and continue to stay in touch. You also need to know how to decline or accept a job offer, and how to respond to a rejection. You'll find sample letters here.

Internships, Externships, and Summer Jobs

There is no essential difference in approach between a cover letter seeking a job and one seeking an internship. If anything, you may want to sell yourself even more, since some internships are very competitive and the experience they offer can be vitally important in your ultimate job hunt. Cover letters can also be used to inquire about externships, which are experiential programs that are generally much shorter-term than internships. Externships often last a week or less, and students frequently participate in them during spring break or over the winter holidays.

College students are accustomed to thinking of years as running from August or September to May or June, with summer an isolated period between school years. Most employers, unless they are in seasonal or tourist-related businesses, don't think in those terms, and typically don't have any reason to take on extra people in the summer. Thus, you will be most successful if you target companies that you know hire summer workers or if you make a good case for why the employer should take you on just for the summer. Be clear about when you're available to work, and for summer slots in high demand, be sure to write early. Check with the employer in the fall to find out when they start interviewing to fill summer slots.

Bonnie Jean Summers
411 Charles Street
Boston, MA 02116
617-555-5878

April 25, 1998

Mr. Rupert Jacobsen
Prudential Securities
711 Sandy Foam Blvd., Suite 100
Locust Valley, NY 11560

Dear Mr. Jacobsen:

With my previous experience working in finance, I would bring more than the average intern to an internship in investments at Prudential.

My education as a finance major at Boston College has also provided me with knowledge and experience in the investment and corporate planning areas of finance. I was a sales assistant at Dean Witter Reynolds, Inc., and I would like to use the solid background of both my education and experience to make a contribution.

I have held various leadership positions that cultivated my organizational and interpersonal skills. I have excellent computer and clerical skills as well.

I would like to speak with you further about a summer internship in your company. I will follow this letter up with a phone call. I look forward to meeting with you.

Thank you for your consideration.

Sincerely,

Bonnie Jean Summers

Allyson Patterson
1405 Tulip Lane
Knoxville, TN 37950
615-555-4050

January 14, 1998

Mr. Demetrius Jones
Jones, Cromwell & Butterfield
111 Magnolia St.
Knoxville, TN 37950

Dear Mr. Jones:

My strong academic background in accounting and information technology will enable me to make a significant contribution in the intern position that Jones, Cromwell & Butterfield advertised in the *Knoxville Journal*.

The accounting field requires discipline and a meticulous concern for detail and organization. My education at the University of Tennessee has prepared me for these demands. My above-average grades and consistently high performance in my major reflect my aptitude for accounting. As you will note on the enclosed resume, I will complete my bachelor's degree in accounting this May.

My internship with a local CPA firm has provided me with the unique skills necessary for working in an accounting firm. I am already equipped and fully trained in making general ledger entries, completing bank reconciliations, and handling payroll data and forms. In addition, I have a working knowledge of tax preparation, estate planning, and depreciation work.

The accounting profession increasingly relies on computers to aid in the preparation and analysis of information. My minor in information technology has provided me with the ability to work efficiently using various accounting systems and software. Furthermore, I possess the technical skills necessary to rapidly familiarize myself with computer systems, thus reducing training time.

I believe you will see from my resume that I am well equipped to fill the position and have both the skills and experience to immediately contribute to the organization. I will contact your secretary in ten days to set up an appointment to meet and further discuss how my background would fit your intern needs. Thank you for your time and consideration.

Sincerely,

Allyson Patterson

Jacquez Holyfield
Box 553
St. Louis University
St. Louis, MO 63166
314-555-1734

March 11, 1998

Dr. Fernando deGracia
Anheuser-Busch
995 Brewery Way
St. Louis, MO 63166

Dear Dr. deGracia:

I am responding to the announcement posted at the St. Louis University business school concerning openings for summer internships at Anheuser-Busch. I would like to be considered for one of these internships.

I understand that five full-time internships are available at your headquarters in St. Louis for the summer of 1998. You may note from my enclosed resume that I have a major in international business. Because I would like to work in the international business field when I graduate in 1998, I would like to have the opportunity to work for the world's leading brewer.

I know that my background, education, and experience will make me an excellent intern for Anheuser-Busch. I am familiar with international business trade, have worked with Texaco International Internship Programs in Santo Domingo, the Dominican Republic, and am bilingual in English and Spanish. I recently read that you will be opening several new offices in Mexico and Costa Rica before the turn of the century.

I understand that you will be visiting St. Louis University the first week in March, and I would be pleased to meet you for an interview. I will contact you next week to schedule an appointment.

Thank you,

Jacquez Holyfield

Mary Hathaway
204 Applegate Drive
Austin, TX 78767
512-555-9894

February 5, 1998

Robert Hamzik
Merrill Lynch Investments
5005 Route 202, Suite 5
Austin, TX 78767

Dear Mr. Hamzik:

My college's career counselor, Lois deJocelyn, who works with you on the county School-to-Work Committee, suggested I contact you about a summer internship at Merrill Lynch Investments. As a junior working toward a Bachelor of Business Administration degree in investment finance, I am ready to make a meaningful contribution to the Merrill Lynch team, gain experience, and develop strong ties to your company.

I am a motivated worker with the right personality to excel in an intern position. I have extensive, high-energy, customer-service experience and a natural ability to surprise people with how hard I work at whatever task I am given to do. I have always loved to make money, as do most people, but I have a knack for making a great deal more than most people through investments in stocks and bonds, along with the ability to choose the most fruitful investment.

In addition to my major in finance, I am completing a minor in information systems. My computer knowledge comes from extensive hands-on experience in MS-DOS, Microsoft Office, Access, and Visual Basic. My classes in programming and work with databases have provided me with excellent skills in these areas.

I've been extremely impressed with the fine work that Merrill Lynch does, and I'm convinced that I can enhance the firm's success. If after reviewing my resume you agree that I can contribute to your company goals, I would like the opportunity to meet with you. I'll phone you next week to make an appointment.

Thank you for your consideration.

Sincerely,

Mary Hathaway

Kristy James
1011 Wood Hollow Road
Cherry Hill, NJ 08034
609-555-1121

March 4, 1998

Ms. Mary Lou Martinez
Customer Service Manager
NationsBank
999 Pine Bluff
Collingswood, NJ 08101

Dear Ms. Martinez:

   My solid academic background, work ethic, and keen attention to detail will make me an excellent addition to your staff as a credit intern. As an accounting student at Drexel University, I am seeking an internship with NationsBank so that I may apply my skills and abilities to benefit your bank.

   My educational experiences will benefit your institution in a number of ways. I have studied managerial accounting, financial accounting, governmental accounting, federal taxation, and managerial finance. Furthermore, I am an information technology minor. By taking these courses, I have been trained to think analytically and to use computers to aid in analyzing data and making decisions. I also have extensive knowledge about how to determine the liquidity and credit-worthiness of a client using financial statements and ratios.

   In addition to my strong background in accounting and information systems, I possess many practical skills. I am well-versed in formal office procedures, including typing, word processing, data entry, and helping clients over the telephone. Last summer, I was on temporary assignment in the accounts payable department at General Electric, where I observed many accounting procedures in action and gained considerable knowledge about private accounting and customer service.

   Finally, I would like to emphasize that I am not only looking for experience this summer, but also for the opportunity to bring my skills and talents to the internship. I will call you early next week to set up an appointment. Thank you very much for your time and consideration.

Sincerely,

Kristy James

Abby Michaels
700 Garland Ave. C-2
Berrien Springs, Michigan 49103
616-555-6834; Fax: 616-555-8876

May 13, 1998

Sarah Sawyer
Staffing Specialist
OptiMax Labs
P.O. Box 10543
Utica, NY 13504

Dear Ms. Sawyer:

Your new sales representative, Jessica Ribiero, mentioned that you might be looking for interns this summer. I am prepared to bring an unusual level of energy, dedication, and hard work to such an internship.

I have worked as an assistant at a photographic studio during school breaks for the past six years, successfully juggling customer service, promotions, public relations, and administrative functions.

This work background is an excellent complement to my solid liberal arts education. I can offer you an eager student with solid computer skills and a keen desire to serve your customers and contribute to the OptiMax team.

Can we pursue this possibility further? I will call within two weeks to verify that you received my resume, answer any preliminary questions you may have, and arrange an appointment to talk about the internship. I look forward to meeting with you to discuss how I can serve OptiMax this summer.

Thank you for your time and consideration.

Cordially,

Abby Michaels

Campus Postal Drop D-13
Colgate University
Hamilton, NY 13346
315-555-7587
E-mail: veddy@neonet.com

September 28, 1998

Matthew Forrest
Internship Coordinator
Equity Advertising Associates
1100 Ackerman Expressway
Oklahoma City, OK 73118

Dear Mr. Forrest:

   The *Internship Bible* indicates that Equity Advertising Associates offers an internship in my hometown of Oklahoma City. As an industrial engineer and a recent graduate of Colgate University with a master's degree in engineering management, I am interested in bringing my business skills to your company. Half of my coursework for both degrees pertained to business and management, and my marketing management directly dealt with advertising. My engineering background makes me particularly well-versed in the software used in advertising.

   Please consider this letter and resume as application to your internship program. I will call you within a week to schedule an interview. I would like to thank you in advance for your time and consideration. I look forward to meeting with you soon.

Yours very truly,

Julia Vedder

Rebekah Charry
Campus Post Box 909
New Jersey Institute of Technology
201-555-9258

March 4, 1998

David Hilton
Human Resources Department
DataQuik
150 JFK Parkway
Short Hills, New Jersey 07078-0999

Dear Mr. Hilton:

My pending Bachelor of Science degree in computer science, along with my UNIX programming and teamwork skills, would enable me to make a significant contribution to the network operations internship you are currently advertising. I have finished the requirements for a degree in mathematics, as well.

My academic background and my leadership positions in campus activities have prepared me for networking and have helped me to hone many of the skills required for this internship. I have experience dealing with the public as a receptionist and a customer-service representative. I acquired computer and network expertise through intensive training at New Jersey Institute of Technology and previous jobs.

I possess the ability and motivation to succeed in this internship and advance your organization's efficiency. My previous employers can assure you that, in addition to my technical abilities, I have the interpersonal skills to fit in with your corporate culture and make my time with your company productive.

I am excited about making a contribution in this internship. Because my skills are an excellent match, I am convinced we should meet so I can demonstrate how I can apply this ability to the network operator internship for our mutual benefit. I will contact you next week to arrange a meeting. In the meantime, should you wish to reach me, you can contact me at 201-555-9258.

Thank you for your time and consideration.

Sincerely,

Rebekah Charry

Lilly Tufts
Box 10102
University of Arkansas
Fayetteville, AR 72701
501-555-6261

15 September 1998

Nancy Nash
Graduate Recruitment Coordinator
Southern Airways
Miami, FL 33101

Dear Ms. Nash:

My solid analytical and problem-solving ability in the theoretical and practical applications of management, human resource management and marketing, along with research and information-gathering techniques would be a considerable asset in the College Internship Program at Southern Airways, which was advertised in a letter I received from the Careers Office at the University of Arkansas. Please find enclosed my resume and academic qualifications for your review.

Currently a junior honors student, I am completing my Bachelor of Business Administration degree, specializing in management, marketing and business strategy. Through group projects and other course work, I have developed the skills to succeed in industries that are customer-oriented and communication intense.

My interest in Southern arises as a result of your preeminent domestic and international standing within the service and airline industry. I seek to intern at a leading company that is customer- and quality-oriented, has a dynamic and challenging environment, where individual and teamwork performance is rewarded, and training and development are part of the company's culture.

Southern has built an enviable reputation based on dedication, commitment, teamwork and a strong desire to succeed in what is a very competitive and continually evolving market. Given my experience, qualities and attitude, I am confident that I will add to Southern's success and would like to request an interview. I will call you by the end of this month to make arrangements.

Thank you for your time and consideration.

Yours sincerely,

Lilly Tufts

Winnie Malloy
1 Deerfoot Trail, Apt. 212
Williamsburg, Virginia 23188
757-555-7138

August 28, 1998

Claudia Halsey
Greenberg, Halsey & Butler
Attorneys-at-Law
111 Silver Circle
Williamsburg, Virginia 23188

Dear Ms. Halsey:

While at the Office of Career Services at the College of William and Mary, I discovered that your firm is offering externships to students interested in pre-law. My background makes me a superior candidate for this position.

My mother is a lawyer, and I have worked in her office for many years. I have also assisted her in various duties such as compiling bankruptcy schedules for her clients, filing, and recording documents, and I once managed her office for three weeks while she was away. Needless to say, this responsibility required a variety of interpersonal and administrative skills.

I can also offer strong research, analytical, and computer skills. I have written many papers for my college courses and have maintained a 3.8 grade point average. Although my computer experience is outlined in my resume, I would like to add that I have owned and worked with computers for many years and have also created my own Web page.

The skills I have acquired through my work experience and through my academic studies are the same skills you are looking for in an extern. I would like the chance to offer you these skills in return for the opportunity to learn more about the legal profession. I am confident that the few days I would spend with you as an extern would be highly rewarding for us both.

To discuss this possibility further, I will contact you early next month. You may alternatively reach me by phone at 757-555-7138. I look forward to speaking with you soon. Thank you for your time and consideration.

Sincerely,

Winnie Malloy

> **Student Applying for Externship**

Kitty Coulter
404 Broadmeadow Rd.
Lexington, KY 40507
606-555-7587

March 2, 1998

Neil Hardy
Marks, Shearson and Westmore
1001 Royal Highway
Lexington, KY 40507

Dear Mr. Hardy:

I spoke with Judge Wiley James last week, and he suggested I contact you regarding the potential opening for a summer clerk position at Marks, Shearson and Westmore. My experience and personal attributes are in direct accordance with your needs, as outlined by Judge James.

My employment experience in the areas of telemarketing and public assistance are ideally suited for a firm such as yours. Combined with my computer and keyboarding expertise, my background would be an immediate asset.

My dependability, diligence, and motivation—qualities recognized and sharpened by previous employers—will allow me to contribute significantly. I believe that my skills, put to work for you, would maximize both quality and profit growth.

I want to make a contribution as a resourceful, competent team player at Marks, Shearson and Westmore, and am looking forward to discussing this clerkship with you. I will be in contact at the beginning of next week to set up an interview.

Thank you for your time and consideration.

Sincerely,

Kitty Coulter

Willem Schmidt
Emsstrasse 3C
49231 Braunschweig, Germany
Tel: (59 5555) 846314
E-mail: z1110068@sw.zr.ut-sb.de

January 29, 1998

Dr. Peter Henninger
New Product Division President
Cornucopia of Canada
66 Dayton Street
Ottawa, Ontario K1A 0M7

Dear Dr. Henninger:

   As a food chemist who has finished his education this year, I am writing you to request information about possible summer employment opportunities at your company. I am interested in a position in product control or product development. Because your first consideration in hiring an applicant should be the skills and services the applicant can provide, I assure you that I offer extensive experience in analyzing food compounds and in using microbiological methods.

   During my final scientific work, I synthesized and purified two substances, liberine and theacrine, which now serve as standards for a GC-MS application in coffee research at the Technical University of Braunschweig.

   I know the food industry often needs to supplement its staff at this time so that you can introduce new products the following spring, and I am available for a term from one to three months starting in June 1998. I am, however, flexible as to the exact dates and length of employment. I also am open to the possibility of continuing my employment while pursuing Ph.D. studies in Canada.

   My knowledge of English is more than adequate for working in your company, and I can speak a little French.

   I will be sponsored by the Work and Travel program of the Council on International Educational Exchange, based in New York. Through this program I will be provided with an Open Employment Authorization of the Canadian Embassy, which entitles me to work legally in Canada.

   Because I will be in Ontario from September 22 to October 13, I would like to arrange an interview during my visit. I will contact you by phone or e-mail to schedule this interview.

   Thank you for your time and consideration. I am looking forward to meeting with you.

Sincerely yours,

Willem Schmidt

Student Applying for Summer Job

Requesting
Informational Interviews

The important thing to remember with informational interview requests is not to mix apples with oranges. You should certainly aim to make a good impression, perhaps flattering the employer, but do not make your letter seem like a fishing expedition for a job. All you are asking for is a small piece of the employer's time so you can find out more about the company and industry.

Pamela Zweidig
104 Sunset Road
Madison, NJ 07940
201-555-9674

October 15, 1998

Roger Budd
Budd Physical Therapy Associates
1005 Route 78
Springfield, NJ 07081

Dear Mr. Budd:

As a junior at Drew University, I start my physical therapy courses next semester. I would like the opportunity to schedule an informational interview with you to learn more about the day-to-day activities of a physical therapist.

I was fascinated with the approach to physical therapy that you described in your recent article in *Physical Therapy Today*, and I felt you would be one of the most enlightening people in the field that I could possibly interview. I know that you are very busy, so I assure you I will be brief. I'd like to give you a call next week to schedule about half an hour of your time at your convenience.

Thank you so much for considering this request.

Cordially,

Pamela Zweidig

Terri Thornfeather
Box 1049
New Mexico State University
Las Cruces, NM 88003

September 5, 1998

Steven Vasiliev
Art Director
Albuquerque Lifestyle
1313 Avenue of the Silver Spur, Suite 4000
Albuquerque, NM 87101

Dear Mr. Vasiliev:

I am student at New Mexico State University, beginning my senior year. Regional magazine publishing has been of interest to me since I took a class in that subject last semester. Your magazine is known as an outstanding example of the small, regional magazine.

My area of concentration in my journalism major is publication design. I would appreciate the opportunity to meet with you and discuss your work and the trends in that field. I am especially interested in your views regarding the manipulation of photographic images. Any insights you have will be greatly appreciated.

I do not intend to take more than about thirty minutes of your time. I will contact your office the week of October 3 to set up a mutually convenient time for this informational meeting.

Sincerely,

Terri Thornfeather

Letters to Your College Career Placement Office

Obviously, you won't need to write a letter to your campus career services or placement office while you're still in school; you can simply enlist its aid by dropping by the office. But if you've graduated and are still unemployed, and assuming you don't live close to your alma mater, you'll want to keep in regular touch with that office by letter. You'll want to keep the office informed of any changes in address, phone number, or e-mail address, and you should also send the office a copy of your resume anytime you update it. You can send routine information updates by e-mail if you wish, but regular mail is a better medium for sending new versions of your resume.

You may not be aware of it, but most colleges and universities have reciprocal agreements that enable the alumni of other universities to use career services facilities at other institutions in other parts of the country. Thus, if you've graduated and moved to a town far from your university, you can often enlist the help of the career services office at the college closest to you. You may need to present a letter from your alma mater requesting the services.

Here's a sample of a letter you might write to your own university's campus career services or placement office:

505 Oriole Street
Baltimore, MD 21203
443-555-7285
E-mail: katydid@baltnet.com

July 14, 1998

Dr. Sylvia Golden
Director of Career Services
Seton Hall University
South Orange, NJ 07079

Dear Dr. Golden:

   I want to thank you again for all the help you gave me in my job search while I was seeking my degree in criminology at Seton Hall. As you know, it has been two months since I graduated, and I unfortunately still have not obtained permanent employment. I have, however, worked fairly steadily for a temp agency, so I've updated my resume to reflect the new skills I've gained there. I'm enclosing the updated version so you can keep it in my file. Please also note my new phone number.

   I know you frequently receive job listings in your office, and I'd like to ask that you let me know of any that are appropriate for me. Feel free to e-mail them to me if that's convenient for you.

   When the recruiting season begins again in the fall, I would appreciate being informed of anyone recruiting in my field. Could you also send me information on your fall Career Expo when it becomes available? I may be in the South Orange area in the fall and would like to combine my travels with some job-hunting if I'm still not employed by then.

   Again, Dr. Golden, thanks for all your help. It's nice to know I can count on my alma mater for continued support. I'll be sure to keep you informed about my job search.

Cordially,

Katy Thompson

> **TIP:** Also keep your favorite professors apprised of your job search and send resume updates after graduation. They often have excellent connections that can prove fruitful for you.

Letters to Recruiters Coming to Your Campus

Sending a letter to a recruiter who is planning a trip to your campus is by no means a standard practice. While the purpose of a cover letter is, of course, to secure an interview, in the campus recruiting process, interviews are secured in a different way. Students generally sign up through their career services office to interview with a recruiter. Frequently more students sign up than there are slots available for interviews, and in that case, recruiters review the resumes and other credentials of the candidates to decide which ones they will interview. Sometimes they choose through a bidding system, or even by lottery.

However, you can get a jump on the competition by finding out at the beginning of the semester which companies are coming to campus, and then calling those companies to find out the name of the recruiter who will be coming to your school. Write a cover letter and send your resume to the recruiter well in advance of his or her visit. Write in a tone that assumes the recruiter will choose you as one of the candidates to interview. The recruiter may be on the road for a long time once recruiting season begins, so allow plenty of time for your letter to reach him or her. You may even want to suggest that the recruiter do an advance phone interview with you. The chances that you are one of those interviewed on campus are greatly increased. Here are two such sample letters.

Joe Mortham
Bates College
Lewiston, ME 04240
206-555-1945

August 29, 1998

David G. Sanders
Sales Manager
Buffco Fitness Products
12884 University Avenue
Providence, RI 02904

Dear Mr. Sanders:

I recently learned that you will be recruiting sales representatives for Buffco Fitness Products on the Bates College campus this fall. Although I plan to submit my resume though the usual screening process, I wanted to introduce myself to you to optimize our time when you come to campus. My sales skills, solid education, and strong interest in the fitness industry qualify me well to sell for Buffco.

I will graduate in December with a Bachelor of Business Administration degree in marketing. I've been a successful sales representative ever since childhood, when I sold chocolate bars door-to-door for little league. I've spent every summer between academic years in a sales job—in fact, I've purposely chosen a different one each year so I could develop a feel for selling a variety of products and services. Since fitness is a great interest of mine and I enjoy working out, I have gravitated to selling fitness products. Buffco products are my favorites; I've had excellent results with them. I am confident that I can sell your products quickly and effectively.

I'd like to suggest a phone interview as a further way to acquaint you with my skills so our time will be well spent when we meet face-to-face on the Bates campus. I'll give you a call next Friday, the 6th, to arrange a time for the phone interview.

I appreciate your consideration, Mr. Sanders. I look forward to talking with you soon and meeting you when you come to campus.

Sincerely,

Joe Mortham

Shawna Banks
Box 1939
Gettysburg College
Gettysburg, PA 17325
717-555-2749

September 2, 1998

Martha Matthews
President and CEO
Cyber Globe Industries
1039 Pilgrim's Highway
Hoboken, NJ 07030

Dear Ms. Matthews:

   I learned through our Career Services Office here at Gettysburg College that you plan to visit our campus this fall to interview candidates for jobs in your international division. I want to make you aware of my interest in one of these positions in advance of your visit here.

   As a French major, I speak the language fluently. I am also reasonably proficient in Russian, Italian, and Portuguese. My minor is in international business, so I am well-versed in global trade and competition. I am widely traveled in Europe and Asia.

   I know you will need savvy managers with international flair to open your overseas plants. My language and interpersonal skills perfectly match your needs in these new areas.

   May we talk over the phone before you visit Gettysburg? I would like to acquaint you with what I have to offer and share some ideas for your global expansion. I will contact you next week to arrange a phone interview. Should you wish to reach me in the meantime, you can reach me at 717-555-2749 during business hours.

Sincerely,

Shawna Banks

Letters Sent Without Resumes

Some career experts, particularly Bob Weinstein, author of *Resumes Don't Get Jobs*, believe that cover letters should be sent out without resumes (in which case they're not really cover letters, since they don't cover anything). He believes that today's resumes look as though they've come off an assembly line and don't convey enough individuality to distinguish one job-seeker from another. He's one of several career experts who contend that a job-search letter can be written in a way so that it does the job of a resume. A letter without a resume may be a bit longer, and instead of simply highlighting some of the experience you would normally list on a resume, it goes into greater detail about your background. Because so many employers who specifically recruit college students have fairly rigid expectations about job-search correspondence, sending a letter without a resume may be risky. I can think of three situations, however, in which the practice could be effective:

- If you did little except study (or party) during your years in college and have virtually no work experience, extracurricular activities, or other material to put on a resume, and your resume would be embarrassingly skimpy if you tried to construct one. A letter may be able to sell you better than a meager, bare-bones resume can.

- If your college career is unusual—if you "took a few years off" between high school and college, if you're a nontraditional student who re-entered school later in life, or if you were established in one career and went back to school to switch to a completely different career.

- If you find you are not getting any nibbles when you send out your traditional cover letter and resume package. When you suspect something may be amiss with your resume, sending your letter out without a resume is a good way to test that theory.

Here's a sample letter that could be sent without a resume:

Paul Brett
5625 Grandview Way
Hanover, NH 03755
603-555-9282

April 9, 1998

George Bennington, CEO
Bennington Industries
19039 Rolling River Industrial Complex
Stamford, CT 06904

Dear Mr. Bennington:

When I read about Bennington Industries's planned expansion into international markets, I came to the immediate conclusion that I could help with this expansion. I will graduate from Dartmouth College next month with a degree in geography and a minor in marketing. I am eager to bring my diverse background to your new international markets in a sales management capacity.

Much of my coursework at Dartmouth focused on international marketing, including advertising on the Internet. I have gained practical experience in this field through work at a local radio station. I took responsibility for market surveys, as well as promotion design and implementation. One of my promotional campaigns won honorable mention in a regional advertising competition.

Before entering Dartmouth, I lived in Mexico City for a year, where I refined my interpersonal skills as executive English teacher at a language institute. I also supervised several other instructors.

I am proficient in a wide range of computer platforms, operating systems, and software programs. My professors and former employers can verify that I am a highly motivated person who consistently takes the initiative when a challenge is presented. I always work hard to see a problem out to its successful resolution.

I would like to have the opportunity to meet with you and discuss how I can contribute to Bennington's international growth and continued success. I will call you in ten days to schedule an interview. If you have questions before then, please contact me at 603-555-9282 during business hours. Thank you for considering me.

Sincerely,

Paul Brett

Follow-Up Letters

If your cover letter has succeeded, you've "closed the sale" and obtained an interview. Just as your cover letter helped shape the employer's impression of you before the interview, your personal demeanor and interview skills shaped that impression during the interview. The lag time between the interview and the moment the hiring decision is made is the time for what a University of Colorado researcher calls "post-interview impression management," in which you maintain and manage the good impression you've made on the employer by following up. A number of follow-up letters and other activities may be appropriate, but the very first one must be the thank-you letter.

The All-Important Thank-You Letter

You must send a thank-you letter right after the interview. At the very latest, send thank-you or follow-up letters by mail within twenty-four hours of an interview. You may even want to ensure that the interviewer has your thank-you letter in hand no later than the end of the next day. You can ensure its timely delivery by faxing, messengering, hand-delivering, sending by overnight delivery, or e-mailing. You may also want to place a quick call to thank the interviewer for his or her time.

If you interviewed with more than one person, you must write a separate thank-you letter to each one. That could mean a lot of work in these days of panel and series interviews, but it must be done. While you can say some of the same basic things in each letter, you should vary the letters a little because the interviewers may very well compare notes.

Assuming that you haven't heard yet from the employer a week after the interview, make another follow-up phone call at the one week or ten day mark.

Why send a thank-you letter after an interview?

- It's just common courtesy. You should always thank people who have given of their time.

- It's a way to keep your name in front of the employer.

- It's a way to stress your fit with the company. It's generally quite effective to say something about the rapport or chemistry you felt with the interviewer. Even if you're stretching the truth, your words may reassure an interviewer who has concerns about your fitting into the team. If a topic came up in the interview that was not job-related but which represents a mutual interest, it doesn't hurt to mention it; such a mention can cement the idea that you will fit into the company culture.

- It's a way to build on the strengths of the interview and emphasize the match between you and the job, especially now that you know more about the company. It's an opportunity to demonstrate that you understand what's really important to the employer, and you can do so by summing up the main points of the interview.

- It's a chance to bring up anything pertinent you thought of after the interview. Did you smack your palm against your forehead as you left the interview, realizing you had forgotten to say something important? The thank-you letter gives you the chance to say it.

- It's a way to address—carefully—anything that went wrong in interview. You can do damage control as long as you don't draw too much attention to the low points of the interview. Damage control may be as simple as assuaging the employer's doubts about your qualifications for the job.

- A thank-you letter can accompany any additional materials (references, transcripts, writing samples) that the interviewer has requested or that you feel might positively affect the hiring decision. Another effective trick is to find a newspaper or magazine article you think the interviewer might appreciate and send a copy along with your thank-you letter. Revealing some of your ideas for the job can also work to your advantage (but don't give away too much).

- It's a way to restate your understanding of the next step in the process. A thank-you letter that reminds the employer what he or she said about the next step in the process is a way of closing the next sale. When you remind the employer that you were told the next step would be a second interview or the opportunity to meet with other important people in the company, you increase your chances that the next step will actually take place.

- The thank-you letter is an opportunity to restate your enthusiasm for the job. Since attitude and enthusiasm are the most important assets a new graduate possesses, you can never express too much enthusiasm. Just as you closed the sale by asking for the interview in your cover letter, you should have closed the sale in the interview by asking for the job. The thank-you letter gives you a chance to again enthusiastically state how much you'd like the job.

- The thank-you letter is another chance to show how well you express yourself. Since we've noted that communications skills are important in nearly every job, it should be clear that every opportunity to show off how well you communicate will bring you closer to a job offer.

- Finally, the most important reason to send a thank-you letter: Most human-resources managers say that fewer than 5 percent of interviewees send thank-you letters, despite the fact that virtually every career book advises sending them. If you send one, you'll distinguish yourself from the other applicants.

Career experts debate what form the thank-you letter should take. Should it be typed or handwritten? A business letter or a social note? Research shows it doesn't matter. It can be a note, a letter, typed, handwritten, faxed, or e-mailed. The only important thing is that you send one.

Here are some examples of thank-you letters:

Thank-you letters that stress a fit with the company

Thank you so much for taking the time to interview me today for the social worker position.

I felt a wonderful rapport not only with you, but with the whole Tappan Zee School Health Clinic staff. I am more convinced than ever that I will fit in beautifully as a member of the team and contribute my skills and talents for the benefit of children in the Tappan Zee district.

I can make myself available for any further discussions of my qualifications that may be needed.

Again, Dr. Page, I very much appreciate you and your staff taking so much time to talk with me about this exciting opportunity.

Notice how the next writer crafts his letter so that Mr. Oswald can easily envision Monday-morning quarterbacking with the candidate about their favorite team around the company watercooler:

I wanted to take the opportunity to thank you most sincerely for taking the time to meet with me about the systems analyst position. After your energetic presentation, I am extremely enthusiastic about the position.

When I walked into your office, I instantly felt as though I belonged at ZygZag Systems. This is the kind of challenge I have been training for throughout my fours years as a computer science major, and I am ready to take it on.

I was excited to discover our mutual interest in the Jacksonville Jaguars. I'm convinced that nothing can stop them from making it to the playoffs this year, aren't you?

Mr. Oswald, I appreciate your time and interest in me, and I look forward to the possibility of playing on your team.

Thank-you letters that build on the strengths of the interview

I'd like to thank you for talking with me about the research assistant position in your seismology lab. I truly appreciate all the time and care you took in telling me about the job and learning more about me.

I'm so pleased that you agree that my senior research project in seismology provides me with excellent experience for this position. I am eager to bring my passion for seismology to the research-assistant position, and I am convinced the knowledge and experience I've already cultivated make me the best researcher for the job.

I very much look forward to learning of your decision soon. Please feel free to contact me if you need more information about my qualifications.

Thank you again for the exhilarating interview.

The next letter is a bit lengthy, but it does a good job of summing up the strengths of the interview and enticing the employer with the idea that this candidate can bring many more ideas and innovations to the workplace:

I want to thank you for taking the time to interview me yesterday for the position of assistant director of the Dayton Sumner Memorial Art Museum. You, Mr. Dawson, and Dr. Acquino exuded warmth, and I know we could all have an excellent working relationship.

As I further studied the job description for the position, I grew even more confident that I could take the museum to new heights of success. With the resources I've gathered, I'm ready to hit the ground running. The 15 percent bonus for attracting grants is an excellent incentive, and I would devote a significant portion of my time to this important venture. I also have a number of great ideas for community and media relations and am excited by your interest in bringing more schoolchildren to the museum.

As I mentioned when we met, I would like to use my fine arts degree and journalism minor to enhance the museum's identity, while at the same time meeting the needs and expectations of the community. I believe I can make a significant contribution to the fundraising effort, and I am particularly interested in exploring a corporate donor program.

I am convinced I could bring a new degree of organization to the museum, and I have ideas about how to make the work space less chaotic and more functional. More importantly, I'd like to get communications on track so that newsletters and invitations are sent out on a timely basis. I have some ideas for making the

newsletter more user-friendly. I feel it is extremely important to maintain close communication between the board and director, and I am committed to doing so.

Ms. Nessen, I thank you again for considering me for this position, and I look forward to the possibility of working with you.

Letter that mentions interview afterthoughts

I'd like to thank you for the time you spent talking with me about the marketing research analyst position you have open at *Razzle* magazine. I am very excited about this position and am convinced that my marketing training equips me more than adequately for the job.

I meant to mention during the interview that last summer I attended a three-week intensive seminar on SPSS, the foremost marketing research software package. I know the job description mentions the ability to use SPSS, and I wanted to make sure you knew that I am extremely well-versed in the use of this software. Please contact me if you have any questions about my ability with this program or about any of my other qualifications.

As you know, my work-study position in the institutional research office here at Emory has provided me with an excellent background for marketing research work.

I look forward to hearing from you soon about the position, and I thank you again for meeting with me.

Thank-you letter that attempts damage control

Thank you for the time you took to interview me for the seminar leader position.

After our interview, I'm convinced that I have the three ingredients you're looking for in your workshop/seminar leaders. I know you expressed some concern in our meeting that I have not worked in a personnel department. I want to stress, however, that I have participated significantly in the hiring process for my sorority and have a solid record of achievement in my human resources classes.

As for your requirement for public-speaking experience, my experience as leader of new student orientation groups at my college for three years and outstanding grades in public-speaking classes qualify me nicely.

Finally, I have enclosed some writing samples to further demonstrate the third requirement, my communications skills.

Thank you again, Mrs. Mellish, for this wonderful opportunity to interview for the seminar leader position. I promise you I won't

let you down if you give me the chance to show what I can do. I eagerly await the next step in the process.

Thank-you letter that accompanies additional materials

Thank you so much for the time you spent interviewing me for the editorial assistant position at the *Bridgewater Courier-News*. I have enclosed the writing samples and list of references you requested.

I think both the samples and references will confirm the skills I spoke of during our meeting. My writing shows an excellent grasp of the English language, and my references will attest to my attention to detail and organizational skills.

I hope you will contact me if you have any questions about my samples or references. I am very much looking forward to taking the next step toward joining the newsroom staff at the *Courier-News*.

In the meantime, Ms. Lyons, thank you again for giving me the opportunity to "strut my stuff" to you.

Thank-you letter that restates an understanding of the next step in the process

It was such a pleasure to meet with you Tuesday about the product manager position at TekTab. I thank you most sincerely for your time in getting to know me and answering all my questions about this exciting position.

Our meeting affirmed to me that this is the right position for me and that I have a great deal to offer your company. Products that make our foods safer are so important right now. My chemistry degree and business minor, combined with the internships I've done for consumer product companies, make me the ideal candidate.

My understanding from our meeting is that the next step is for me to meet with your Vice President for Research and Development, Dr. Fairchild. I can meet with her any time it's convenient and am very much looking forward to speaking with her.

Mr. Miller, I am truly grateful for the opportunity to meet with you, and I look forward to hearing from you soon about a meeting with Dr. Fairchild.

Thank-you letter that restates enthusiasm for the job

Thank you for taking the time to meet with me about what I did last year in my work-study position in the admissions office. I cannot tell you how excited and enthusiastic I am about the possibility of parlaying my admissions experience into a full-time position at my alma mater after graduation.

I really enjoyed talking with you and hearing about your plans for your tour of duty as dean of student life. I was truly impressed with your ideas, especially since you have developed them so early into the job.

I know you are not sure if the budget will allow you to offer me this position. I look forward to talking with you again once the picture becomes more clear. I will be traveling from August 3rd through the 15th. If I haven't heard from you before I leave, I'll give you a call while I'm on the road.

Please know that my priority is to serve my alma mater. I cannot think of a more appropriate way to show my appreciation to the university for the wonderful education I've received.

Dr. Sussman, thanks again for talking with me and for considering how I might be of service to the admissions office. I very much want this position and know I can succeed in it.

Thank you letter after an interview at a career fair

Many companies are cutting costs by doing less recruiting at individual colleges and more at career fairs. Thus, the career fair is becoming an increasingly important component of the college student's job search. Not many college job-seekers send thank-you letters after interviews at job or career fairs, so you can make a real impression if you do. Imagine how you'll stand out among the dozens of students who meet with recruiters at job fairs if you're the only one who writes a thank-you note.

Thank you very much for taking the time to meet with me at the Central Michigan Career Fair today. I certainly appreciate your time and attention in the midst of so many students seeking jobs.

You were extremely thorough in explaining PlazTec's management trainee program. Now that I have a better idea what the position entails, I am even more certain that I would be an outstanding member of your team. My solid education in management and the fact that I have worked my way through college show a strong work ethic and determination, two qualities you said were essential to success at PlazTec.

I would like the opportunity to visit the PlazTec headquarters and speak to you further about the management trainee program. I'll contact you early next week to arrange an appointment to talk further.

Mr. Bennett, thanks again for your time and attention.

Thank-you letter following interview with on-campus recruiter

Career expert Brian Krueger recommends hand-delivering a thank-you note to the recruiter you've interviewed with on campus before the recruiter leaves the campus for the day.

> Thanks so much for talking with me today about the position in fashion merchandising at Holbrook's. I was truly inspired by the energy and dedication you brought to our interview.
>
> I am positive that I have what it takes to bring the same kind of energy and dedication to your company. As I mentioned, Holbrook's has been my first choice for fashion since before I was a pre-teen. I bought the suit I wore to our interview at Holbrook's!
>
> My education has equipped me for this job, and my enthusiasm will ensure my success. My internships with several local apparel stores have taught me a great deal about meeting the needs of target market segments.
>
> I would like to take the next step in this process and discuss the position further with you at your office in the Long Beach store. I plan to contact your secretary on Friday to schedule a mutually convenient time to meet.
>
> Again, Ms. Stilwell, I thank you most sincerely for your time, your energy, and the inspiration you gave me to launch my career at Holbrook's.

Following up After Rejection

One of the cruel realities of job hunting is that you will receive rejection letters. Sometimes you'll be crushed to received a rejection letter after you've interviewed for a position, but other times, you'll get the dreaded "thanks-but-no-thanks" letter before you've even had the opportunity to interview. Just about no one writes a follow-up letter after getting a rejection without an interview. But that's a good reason to do it. You'll stand out because no one else does it. It's another chance to put your name before the employer. And because your approach is unique, the employer may very well remember you the next time there's an opening. This kind of letter can be very short and sweet. It won't take up much of your time, but it just might pay off someday.

> Thank you for your letter of September 12. I was, of course, disappointed to learn I had not made the list of finalists for the sales position you are filling.
>
> Since I remain confident that I have the skills and qualifications to excel in your company, I hope you will consider me for any similar positions either now or in the future. I admire Sticky

Wickets, Inc., very much and will certainly contact you the next time I learn of an opening for which I'm qualified.

Thank you again for considering my qualifications.

More common is the follow-up letter after you've been rejected following an interview. Here's an example of how you can respond:

Thank you for letting me know you had decided to hire someone else for the programming position I interviewed for. I was disappointed that I did not get the position, but I very much appreciate the time and concern you and your staff took to talk with me and show me around your headquarters.

I hope you'll keep my materials on file and consider me for future vacancies. I know yours is a growing company, so I'm convinced a position will turn up before long for which I am a perfect fit. If any other departments or regional offices have openings, I would appreciate hearing about them.

Again, Ms. Neeson, thank you so much for all the time and thought you put into considering me for this position.

The What-Did-I-Do-Wrong Letter

If your stack of rejection letters is growing larger, it's possible that something about your interviewing style is causing you to be screened out of the process. If you feel like you're spinning your wheels, you have little to lose by trying to find out if you are doing something wrong. Choose an interviewer with whom you felt you had particularly good rapport. The interviewer is certainly under no obligation to respond to your request for feedback, but if he or she really is someone with whom you had good chemistry, the interviewer may help you out. Be aware, too, that you may get better results if you phone to ask what you did wrong. The interviewer will be disarmed and more likely to respond. It's even possible that you are being rejected based on a misunderstanding—some sort of mistaken perception that you don't meet the qualifications for the job. If that's the case, you could get back into the running simply by reconnecting and asking what you did wrong. Here's a sample what-did-I-do-wrong letter:

Thank you for this week's letter informing me that you have offered the budget analyst position to someone else. Naturally, I was disappointed, but I do thank you for interviewing me and considering me for the position.

Ms. Nesbitt, I felt a very strong connection with you in our interview and wondered if I might ask you a big favor. Since my qualifications perfectly match those in the job description, I am concerned that I do not interview well. Could I trouble you to

critique my interview performance and tell me what I could have done better to capture this job?

Again, I appreciate the time you took to interview me, and I would be most grateful if you could provide feedback on my interviewing.

Letter to Accept a Job Offer

Awesome! You got the offer! Even if you've accepted a job offer over the phone, it's important to write a formal acceptance letter. Stating in writing your understanding of the terms of employment will help clear up any misunderstandings before they can snowball. Your acceptance letter is not a contract, but if any legal question ever arises over the terms of your employment, it certainly cannot hurt to have your understanding of those terms in writing. Here's a sample acceptance letter:

It was certainly wonderful news when you called this afternoon to offer me the position as assistant buyer for Goldenrod's. Please consider this letter my formal acceptance.

I am pleased to accept your offer at a salary of $29,000 annually. As we agreed, my starting date will be July 28 to enable me to finish a summer computer class that will enhance my skills for Goldenrod's.

I also understand that I will receive full company pay and benefits during the twelve-week training program and that I am considered probationary during that time.

Thank you again, Mr. Shaw, for offering me this wonderful opportunity, and do let me know if I can do anything in advance of my start date to facilitate the paperwork, or if there are any areas you'd like me to be reading up on.

What a delight it will be to work with you and the Goldenrod's team!

Letter to Decline an Offer

If you find yourself in the enviable position of receiving more than one job offer, you would be wise to write a nice letter to the employer you didn't choose, informing the company of your decision. After all, things might not work out at your chosen company. A year from now, I hope your first-choice company won't decide you weren't what they were looking for, but if they do, or you decide you hate working there, you may wish to approach your rejected suitor again. If you've left things with them on a cordial note, they will be more likely to welcome you back.

I want to thank you for offering me the financial analyst position at Royalco, as well as for the time you and you team spent with me during the interview process.

Because I was so impressed with Royalco, I had a very difficult decision to make as I weighed offers. After much thought and careful consideration, I have elected to accept another company's offer.

I wish Royalco the best continued success.

Thank you again, Ms. Petersen, for all your time and effort. Perhaps our paths will cross again someday.

Graduate School Application Letters

I've included a few sample graduate school application letters because students sometimes decide that they would benefit from a graduate degree instead of a job right out of school. Some of my students have said they wished *Dynamic Cover Letters* included some samples of grad school letters. Sending a cover letter with your application is usually not required, but it can be your key to making a great first impression. It's a way to distinguish yourself from other applicants, sell yourself to the director of your prospective graduate program, and provide an extra sample of your writing for your application file, especially since writing skills are so important in graduate school. As with an employment cover letter, a graduate school application letter should focus on what you can do for the school rather than what the school can do for you.

Theo Vincent
Campus Box 0085
College of Wooster
Wooster, OH 44691

March 21,1998

Kathy Roman
Dean of Admissions
The Ohio State University College of Law
Drinko Hall
55 West 12th Street
Columbus, OH 43210

Dear Ms. Roman:

   I am writing to request admission into the Ohio State University College of Law's Class of 1997. Having worked with College of Law graduates Jean Clausen and H. Wheeler Rogers, I have experienced first-hand the skill of the attorneys Ohio State produces. Given the opportunity, I intend to be as highly respected as they are.

   I will graduate this spring from the College of Wooster with a bachelor's degree in investment finance and a minor in information technology. During my undergraduate studies, I demonstrated my strong work ethic by holding two jobs to cover my college expenses while maintaining a 3.7 grade-point average. I exhibited an early interest in law by spending the summer after my freshman year working as an office assistant in a law firm.

   I am a hard-working and driven individual who can contribute immensely to the continued success and reputation of the College of Law.

   Ms. Roman, thank you for considering my credentials. I will contact you in a week to confirm your receipt of my application.

Sincerely,

Theo Vincent

Randall Adams
99 Berkeley Street
Stamford, CT 06904
203-555-9528

March 19, 1998

Dean James Kane
Director of Graduate Studies
College of Business Administration
University of South Carolina
Columbia, SC 29208

Dear Dean Kane:

I possess a wide range of research and teaching abilities, which I would like to contribute to the University of South Carolina's College of Business Administration as a doctoral student. Please accept and carefully consider the enclosed application to your Ph.D. program in business administration and management.

Currently, I am market research manager at *Business Month* magazine, and, as you can see on the attached resume, I have worked for several years in marketing and media research. I earned a Bachelor of Science degree in marketing from Syracuse University and a Master of Arts in Journalism and Communications degree in magazine publishing from the University of Florida. I also have several years of teaching experience. I taught while obtaining my master's degree, and I am currently an adjunct professor of advertising.

My goal is to conduct meaningful research in the field and teach management and marketing at the college level. While pursuing that goal I would like to benefit the University of South Carolina by conducting academic research and teaching.

I offer myself as a strong researcher and teacher with considerable energy and ambition, as well as enough years of "real world" experience to be able to blend theory with real life experiences.

I look forward to learning of the admissions committee's decision regarding my application. Thank you for your consideration.

Sincerely,

Randall Adams

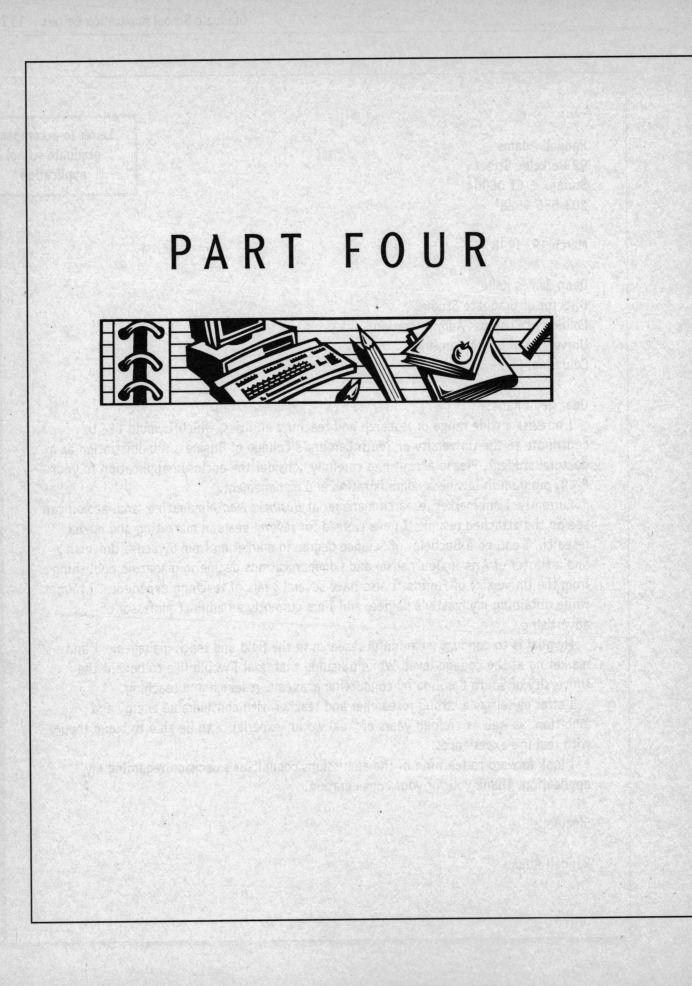

PART FOUR

Sending Your Cover Letter into Cyberspace: The Internet Job Hunt

The Internet is playing an ever-increasing role in people's job hunts, especially those of savvy college students. While it is not possible in this space to explain to a novice (or "newbie," in Internet parlance) all the technical issues and protocols involved in using the Internet or mounting a full-blown Internet job-search, this section will tell you about six basic ways to use your cover letter on the Internet.

Six Ways to Use Your Cover Letter on the Internet

All the World Wide Web sites discussed in this chapter can be accessed through a site I'm involved with at Stetson University. Since Internet addresses tend to go out of date rather quickly, visiting this umbrella site will not only enable you to keep up with changes, but will also help you learn a great deal about conducting an Internet job search:

The Quintessential Career and Job-Hunting Resources Guide

http://www.stetson.edu/~rhansen/careers.html

Taking Advantage of Resume Databases

The World Wide Web component of the Internet contains numerous databases that allow you to submit your resume. Some databases are open to all job-seekers, while others target a particular demographic, geographic, or industry group. Similarly, some databases charge a fee for the privilege of listing your resume there, while others are free. The idea is that employers can access and search these databases using keywords. When they find resumes that match what they're searching for—bingo! The person behind the resume—you—just might be contacted for an interview. Keep in mind that this method of job-hunting is too new to be relied upon as a sure-fire way to find a job. Some of my students have had several responses when they've submitted material to these databases; others have had none. Experts advise that you not spend more than a quarter of your total job-search time on Internet methods. However, if you are in the computer field or another high-tech industry, you can expect better results and may want to spend as much as half your job-search time on the Internet.

Some databases have templates you fill in to submit your resume; others ask you to paste your resume in text format onto a particular part of a submission form on a Web page. Currently, a limited number of no-fee databases provide an option for also submitting cover letters. Those that do include:

- CareerWeb: http://www.cweb.com/register/
- The Monster Board: http://www.monster.com/
- Online Career Center: http://www.occ.com
- E-Span: http://www.espan.com

Whenever you see an option to submit your cover letter to a resume database, don't pass it up. You are providing many more opportunities for the database's search engine to turn up keywords, as well as showing employers how well you express yourself. It's an extra chance to sell yourself. You have to focus on your own qualifications and assets because you can't target this type of letter to a specific company or position, but you can and should be very specific about what type of position you seek and how you can benefit an employer.

Responding to Online Ads

Job listings are plentiful on the Internet. Just as databases of resumes are available for employers to search, databases of job listings are accessible to job-seekers to search. You can tap into many of these through the Quintessential Career and Job-Hunting Resources Guide. You can also find job listings on the Web pages of individual companies. Applicants are usually asked to respond to online ads or job listings via e-mail.

Employers expect that e-mail responses to job listings will include cover letters. Since you are responding to a specific company, your electronic cover letter will be much like a print cover letter that responds to an ad. You should tailor your letter specifically to the ad and demonstrate your knowledge of the company.

Using the ResumePATH Web Site

This Web site (http://www.bridgepath.com/getajob/resumepath/cfm) enables you to zap your resume and cover letter off to more than 200 companies, including Microsoft, Smith and Barney, Bank of Boston, and Deloitte Consulting. You can choose companies based on field or industry, or you can send your materials to all the companies. This method defies all the rules about tailoring your cover letters to each position, because the same cover letter (and resume) goes out to all the selected companies. Using this method is therefore analogous to the cover letter no-no of mass-mailing the exact same letter to hundreds of companies. But the difference is that it is so much easier and cheaper (free, to be precise) to send your resume and cover letter to multiple companies through the Internet than it is to send hard copies through the mail that even if the response you get is low, you have wasted little time, minimal effort, and no money.

Knowing that your cover letter will go to many diverse companies, be as specific as you can about what you want to do without limiting yourself too much. Focus on your qualifications and attributes since you can't focus on individual companies. You can do some degree of tailoring if you send a different cover letter to the companies in each of the available ResumePATH fields.

Creating Your Own Web Page

Since many universities now have either regular classes or smaller seminars on Web page creation, you can learn to develop and promote your own page to employers. An added bonus is that Web design skills are highly marketable in themselves. In addition to your resume and samples of your work, you can also place a cover letter on your page. As with some of the other Internet techniques discussed in this chapter, the cover letter you publish on your page cannot be tailored to any one position. Therefore, it should stress your qualifications and be very clear about what you want to do and what you can contribute to prospective employers. To find out how to obtain Web publishing privileges at your college, check with your campus system administrator.

Responding to Print Ads with E-Mail

Sometimes employers give you the option of responding via e-mail to ads they've placed in print. If you have a choice between sending a print version or sending e-mail, which should you send? Both! Send e-mail for its immediacy, but note in the e-mail that you will follow up with a hard copy of your cover letter and resume. E-mail is not only a quick way to respond, but also a way to show off your Internet savvy, a skill that might be important in the job. And just like "snail mail," e-mail occasionally fails to reach its destination, so it's wise to send a printed copy as a backup.

Even when companies don't provide an e-mail address, they often direct you to their Web page so you can learn more about the company and position. Always take advantage of these opportunities, because the more information you have, the better targeted your cover letter will be.

Posting Your Cover Letter to a Usenet Newsgroup

Usenet is its own unique corner of the Internet. Usenet consists of thousands of special-interest groups, some so specialized you wonder if they could really have any participants. Most Usenet groups function as interactive discussion groups in which a message sent to the group will be disseminated to everyone who subscribes to that group. Many job-related Usenet groups are essentially one-way groups. Just as the World Wide Web houses resume databases and job-listings databases, Usenet contains newsgroups that function in much the same way. Some entire newsgroups exist as repositories of resumes that employers can look through, while others are filled with job listings that job-seekers can peruse.

Some people who post their resumes on Usenet newsgroups post cover letters; some don't. Should you? Yes. It's an opportunity to market yourself to employers and show off your writing skills. If you don't know how to subscribe to and post messages to Usenet newsgroups, ask the system operator at your university, because not all colleges support Usenet. Be careful about which newsgroups you post to. The guardians of the groups are wary of messages that are not relevant to their group's theme, and Usenet is loosely governed by a special set of etiquette rules, so try to familiarize yourself with those rules before posting your cover letter and resume to any particular group.

Guidelines for posting your cover letter on the Internet

- Brevity is particularly important. For some readers, a screen of e-mail seems equivalent to a page of type, yet an e-mail screen is generally even smaller than your monitor's screen. It is probably unrealistic to think you can squeeze a substantive cover letter on a single e-mail screen, but you don't want the reader to have to scroll through multiple screens. Make your letter long enough to sell yourself, but keep it concise.

- Use text (ASCII) format for both your cover letter and resume.

- Unlike most word-processing programs, some e-mail programs don't have spell-checker features, so it's especially important to proofread your cover letter carefully before you send it into cyberspace. You can also compose your letter in a word-processing program (which can then serve as your follow-up hard copy), spell-check it, and then copy and paste it in text format into an e-mail message.

- Despite the formatting limitations of your e-mail text, which can't be italicized, underlined, centered, or made bold, you can still enhance the readability of your online cover letter with bullets created out of lower-case letter o's, plus signs (+), dashes (—), and asterisks (*).

- Don't send your cover letter and resume separately. Send them as one unified e-mail message.

- Keywords are especially important in your e-mailed cover letter because search engines will pick up on them when the employer looks for candidates who meet the company's criteria. See "Packaging and Mailing," page 37, for more information about keywords.

- Create and store a standard cover letter in your e-mail program that you can adapt for each position you apply for.

For more information about Internet basics and job-hunting on the Internet, consult these helpful sources:

- Bounds, Shannon and Arthur Karl. *How to Get Your Dream Job Using the Internet.* (Scottsdale, AZ: Coriolis Group Books, 1996.)

- Jandt, Fred E. and Mary B. Nemnich. *Using the Internet and the World Wide Web in Your Job Search.* (Indianapolis: JIST Works, Inc., 1997.)

- Riley, Margaret. *The Guide to Internet Job Searching.* (Lincolnwood, IL: VGM Career Horizons, 1996.)

PART FIVE

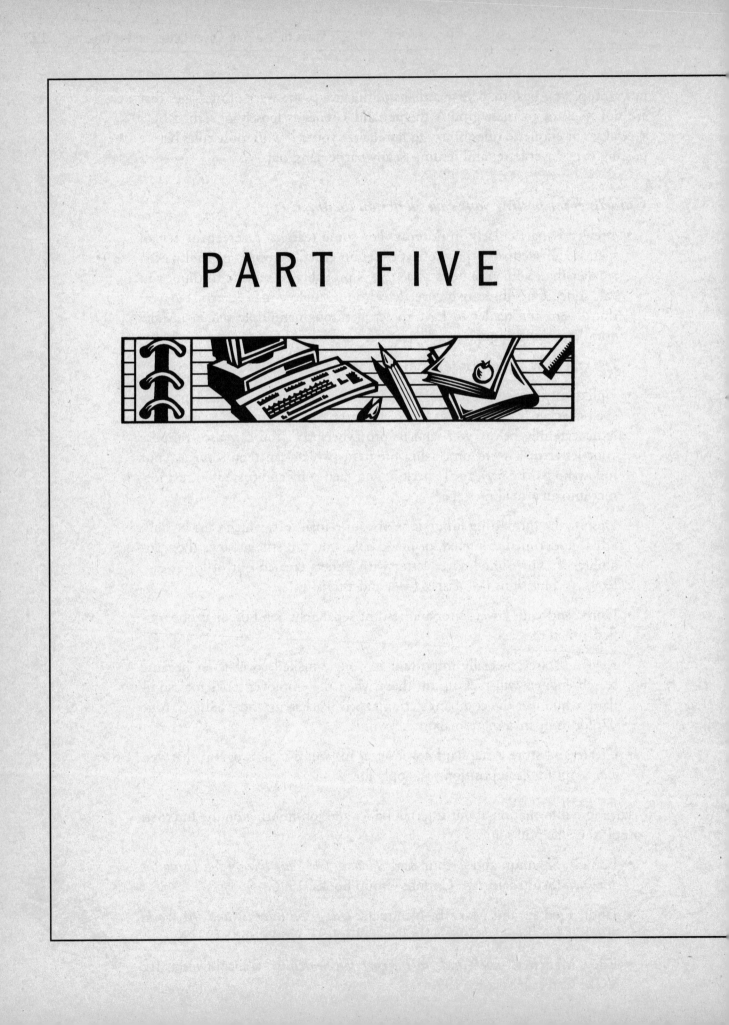

Sample Letters for New Grads Seeking Today's Hottest Jobs

These samples are here to give you inspiration and food for thought. When you see a letter written by someone in the same major as yours seeking a similar career, you may get some ideas for your cover letter that you didn't have before, but do remember this book's earlier words about formulaic cover letters. If every new graduate used chunks of these sample letters wholesale, all their letters would sound alike. So lift a phrase here and there, copy the structures if you wish, and emulate the tone of the letters, but don't use these letters in their entirety, substituting only your name and personal information. It's unethical to plagiarize these letters, and it could be dangerous. Think of the most popular jobs students at your college apply for, and imagine how recruiters might react if a hundred students wrote virtually the same letter.

Tara Fenimore
555 Campus Row
Wellesley, MA 02181
617-555-1983

April 30, 1998

Dawn Hughes
Vice President
Pinnacle Training Seminars
19984 Commonwealth Avenue
Boston, MA 02116

Dear Ms. Hughes:

My pending degree in English, along with my solid ability to express myself persuasively, verbally and in writing, will enable me to add value to a position as a seminar trainer with Pinnacle. My talent for adapting language for various audiences and presenting material freshly and effectively would be exceptionally useful in a trainer position.

I will graduate *summa cum laude* from Wellesley College in June, having won several major honors for forensics and public speaking. Observers frequently tell me that I am unusually articulate. I am excited about the possibility of bringing my language and presentation skills to a company I respect as much as Pinnacle.

Having studied Pinnacle's achievements with admiration, I am aware that success at Pinnacle depends on the trainer's ability to convince seminar attendees to enroll in in-depth training programs. I've used my talent for holding an audience's attention to successfully sell household items every summer during my college years. Each summer, I surpassed my sales of the summer before, and last year achieved the highest sales of any collegiate salesperson.

I can think of no better way to demonstrate my presentation skills than meeting with you to "sell myself." Please permit me to call you by the end of the month to set up a time when I may prove what an asset I will be to Pinnacle. If you'd like to talk with me before that time, you are welcome to call me during business hours at 617-555-1983, where voicemail can take your message in the event I'm not available.

Ms. Hughes, thank you so much for taking the time to review my qualifications.

Cordially,

Tara Fenimore

Camryn Swink
2507 Owlwood Court
Kalamazoo, MI 49007
616-555-1823

September 15, 1998

Dean Margaret Merryfield
Kalamazoo College
Kalamazoo, MI 49007

Dear Dean Merryfield:

I was excited to learn from the Career Services Office that you are seeking a multilingual admissions counselor to help recruit students to Kalamazoo. As a new graduate with a bachelor's degree in French and a minor in Spanish, I am well qualified to take on this new position. In addition, I have a reading knowledge of German and Russian, as well as enormous enthusiasm for my alma mater. My facility with languages and intimate knowledge of Kalamazoo would give me a distinctive edge as your new international admissions counselor.

Because of my long-standing interest in other languages and cultures, I have traveled extensively under the Youth Hostel program. My experience interacting with young people from many nations would provide an advantage in interviewing students of various nationalities.

I have received several academic distinctions for my ability to communicate using written foreign languages, a skill that would enable me to help adapt the college's educational programs, publicity, and marketing materials to the cultural background of the international student audience and target the students' cultural preferences.

I'm sure you'll agree that interviewing me would be advantageous. Since I visit campus frequently, I'll stop by and see Barbara, the admissions receptionist, next week to see if I can arrange an interview. Please don't hesitate to call me at 616-555-1823 if you'd like to speak with me sooner. Dean Merryfield, I'm grateful to you for considering my application.

Cordially,

Camryn Swink

Douglas Gregory
Campus Postal Drawer 5A
Knox College
Galesburg, IL 61401
309-555-9274

February 25, 1998

Ronald Goffredi
Managing Director
New World Consolidated
595 Broadway Blvd.
Milwaukee, WI 53201

Dear Mr. Goffredi:

I have long admired New World's practice of hiring graduates with solid liberal arts backgrounds for management trainee positions. In fact, it was with New World in mind that I became a philosophy major. I will graduate next month and am prepared to bring my critical thinking, problem solving, and communications skills to New World's management trainee program.

The abilities I've developed during my college career align extremely well with the skills New World seeks in its management trainees. As a philosophy honors student, I've learned to digest and summarize large amounts of complex information, present ideas—both orally and in writing—in an organized and coherent fashion, reshape ideas in light of new circumstances, and ask creative questions to stimulate discussion. My research of New World tells me these are exactly the skills that can drive us to mutual success.

Having earned my way through college through a series of responsible jobs, I've also demonstrated a strong work ethic. I also displayed teamwork and a competitive drive through my co-captainship of the varsity soccer team. I am confident that I have the "right stuff" to make my mark in your management trainee program, and I am eager to meet with you to review my suitability as a New World employee. May I call you next week to schedule an appointment? Thank you for including me in your applicant pool.

Sincerely,

Douglas Gregory

Jennifer Trinkle
Box 8284
Northwestern University
Evanston, IL 60208
847-555-2395

June 15, 1998

Dorothy Manheim
Director of Consumer Affairs
City of Chicago
1115 Wacker Drive
Chicago, IL 60601

Dear Ms. Manheim:

I'm interested in bringing the fresh insights of a new psychology graduate to the advertised position of assistant director of consumer affairs. I recently graduated with honors with a Bachelor of Science in psychology from Northwestern University. My senior research thesis centered around consumer behavior in urban populations.

My psychology studies have provided me with the ability to deal effectively with people, as well as with great insight into consumer psychology. The many group projects I've engaged in during college have taught me a great deal about promoting good relationships within a group and in the community. Several research classes have enabled me to develop solid interviewing techniques in investigative, reporting, and marketing research contexts. I have also taken several marketing courses, including one in consumer behavior.

I am cognizant that this job requires solid knowledge of statistical methods and computers, and I am well qualified. My knowledge covers most platforms, operating systems and software programs, including the major statistical packages.

I am most eager to meet with you and share my ideas about this position. I plan to contact your office on July 1 to schedule a time to meet. Please also feel free to reach me at 847-555-2395.

Please accept my appreciation for your consideration of my qualifications.

Sincerely,

Jennifer Trinkle

Dennis Brown
Campus Box 7274
Franklin and Marshall College
Lancaster, PA 17604
717-555-6319

April 14, 1998

Mr. John Jameson
Vice President, Human Resources
Research Development
1405 Locust Street
Philadelphia, PA 19104

Dear Mr. Johnson:

   As a graduating senior from Franklin and Marshall College, I am seeking a position in your law studies department where I can make a positive contribution to your firm. As a sociology major, I have undertaken a one-year comprehensive research project on the topic of capital punishment. This project involved a self-administered questionnaire, data analysis, the application of sociological theory, and statistical methods, using the latest research software. I also hold a minor in business law and am accustomed to briefing cases, researching decisions, and exploring recent issues concerning law.

   These skills and experiences align perfectly with a position at Research Development. Your company has a reputation for excellence as well as precision, and I know that my combination of education, interest, and motivation will make me a real contributor in your law studies department. I will contact you within a week to arrange a meeting at your earliest convenience. If you have any questions before then you can contact me at 717-555-6319.

Sincerely,

Dennis Brown

Polly Danielsen
1101 West Bridle Trail
Danville, VA 24541
804-555-9293

September 4, 1998

Charles Devere
Senior Analyst
The Pierpont Foundation
570 Second Street, NW
Washington, DC 19982-4242

Re: Research Analyst Position

Dear Mr. Devere:

Having graduated from Princeton University this May with a degree in religious studies, I am confident that I have the research and critical-thinking skills required to meet your needs. Please accept this letter and my enclosed resume as application for the research analyst position that was posted on the Pierpont Foundation's job announcement board.

My interest in research began in college when I undertook a major research project in my comparative religions class. This interest led to an internship with the National Ecumenical Council, where I began assisting others in research on a questionnaire study for the Women's Programs Office. After I was there for only two weeks, my supervisors recognized my initiative and abilities to the extent that they entrusted me with sole responsibility for a research project. The data I presented and compiled, which were collected from a survey concerning women's representation in the clergy, was introduced at a Committee on Women in the Clergy meeting.

I would greatly appreciate an opportunity to discuss with you further my candidacy for the research analyst position because I know I can do a good job for you. I will call you to arrange an interview at your earliest convenience.

Enthusiastically yours,

Polly Danielsen

Ga Kim Le
6239 Spruce Street, Apartment B5
Philadelphia, PA 19104

International Relations
Major

January 13, 1998

Ms. Jessica Aguilero, Associate
International Consultants, Inc.
9772 Broad Street, 7th Floor
New York, NY 10004

Dear Ms. Aguilero:

   I am currently a senior at the University of Pennsylvania majoring in international relations. I am writing to express my interest in position of Field Associate at your firm. Talking with various alumni, such as your colleague Frances Potter, and your representatives from International Consultants, Inc., I am very impressed by significant responsibilities offered to its employees and ample opportunities to excel in career for entrepreneurial, achievement-oriented type of person. More importantly to me, your firm's global presence is particularly well-suited to my background.

   More than three semesters of study abroad and work experience in one of the most recently emerging markets — Vietnam — has provided me with exceptional experiences and strong connections with entrepreneurs to decision-making officials in the private and public sectors. Participating on a small team to reorganize several Vietnamese small businesses virtually from scratch at a very young age, I was thrilled by the overwhelming challenges, yet excited to exercise my leadership skills. The result exceeded all expectations; not only did we stabilize the businesses, but we also managed to establish an international presence for them on the World Wide Web.

   Equipped with leadership and interpersonal skills enhanced by education from one of the world's top universities, and bolstered by unique experiences, I am confident that I can contribute significantly to your implementation of globalization strategy, particularly in emerging markets.

   I would greatly appreciate the opportunity to be included on your interviewing schedule. I will follow up this letter with a phone call to check on my status. Thank you very much for your consideration.

Sincerely,

Ga Kim Le

Shawn Sebring
P.O. Box 4927267
Syracuse, NY 13244
315-555-1937

History Major

October 25, 1998

Kenneth Alexander
Chief Legislative Aide
New York State Department of Urban Development
Albany, NY 12201

Dear Mr. Alexander:

There is nothing quite like bringing a historical perspective to solving New York's contemporary urban challenges. That's the unique angle that I, as a recent history graduate, would bring to the legislative analyst position you currently have open. Having spent a semester in an internship in your department, I know that legislative analysts must be able to track trends and predict shifts in political views, monitor changes in government policies, manage information, collect and evaluate data, and use statistical methods and software programs to analyze the results of research. These tasks are all in a day's work for a hard-working history major like me. I have developed and overseen numerous research projects while pursuing my bachelor's degree in history from Syracuse University.

I am convinced that my history background will provide me with a distinct advantage in this position because it has enabled me to identify key questions involved in the issues, weigh evidence and opinions, and reach conclusions. I've also demonstrated excellent writing skills that will allow me to document conclusions and present them clearly.

I have also functioned effectively as a research assistant to several professors in the history department, employing skills that align remarkably well with those listed in the job description for the legislative analyst position. I was captain of the university varsity lacrosse team, enabling me to develop teamwork and leadership skills that will serve me exceedingly well in this position.

I hope you'll agree that an interview would benefit both of us. I plan to contact your office next week to schedule an appointment. Please contact me at 315-555-1937 if you have any questions.

I want to thank you for considering me for this position.

Sincerely,

Shawn Sebring

Flynn Daniels
Campus Box 29293
Wake Forest University
Winston Salem, NC 27109
910-555-6626

January 18, 1998

Joanne Johnson
Human Resources Manager
Andersen Consulting
1001 South Beach Way
Miami, FL 33101

Dear Ms. Johnson:

   I recently learned that Andersen Consulting is looking for an energetic and dynamic person, capable of thinking creatively, who also possesses experience in business and finance. I am eager for a career in management consulting and am interested in discussing with you how my skills are of value to your organization.

   My immersion into the world of business and finance as an intern at Global Financial Advisors has provided valuable preparation for business consulting. As a twenty-year-old who regularly cold-called CEOs and the owners of successful Atlanta corporations to persuade them to meet with me, I banked my success on the ability to think creatively, conceptualize on many levels, and communicate crisply. I effectively explained the value my firm could provide and demonstrated my competency in the tax, legal, insurance, and investment realms. I helped clients understand complex ideas in simple terms, motivated them to action, and then cooperated with a team of Global associates to implement our ideas.

   My wide-ranging college career has provided me with a combination of skills and experience that are well-suited to the challenges of consulting. My senior ecology thesis involved extensive research, and required me to convey my ideas concisely in an oral presentation and a comprehensive treatise. Several leadership positions in a variety of activities throughout my years at Wake Forest demanded that I organize my time and resources efficiently, and assist others to do the same.

   My distinctive background has well equipped me with tools that will make me valuable to Andersen.

   I would like the opportunity to discuss with you further how my abilities can best benefit your organization. I look forward to speaking with you when I call during the first week in February to arrange a time to meet. Thank you for your time and consideration.

Sincerely,

Flynn Daniels

Matt Bryan
7010 Melville Drive, Apt. 103
Maple Grove, MN 55369
999-555-3888

November 13, 1998

Janis Mathis
Chairperson
Rovinsky, Inc.
800 Third Street Square
Minneapolis, MN 55415

Dear Ms. Mathis:

John Lunde suggested I contact you about openings for Geographic Information Systems (GIS) consultants at Rovinsky, Inc. My recent internship experience and academic background fit remarkably well with the requirements of the position.

I will graduate in December from the University of Wisconsin at Eau Claire. I am a geography-cartography major with a graphic communications minor. Currently I am completing an internship with Roswell County in the Department of Research and Evaluation. This experience has given me hands-on knowledge of how GIS plays a role in the workplace. I have used Arcview GIS during this internship, as well as Atlas GIS in the past, and have begun to learn ArcInfo as well. This internship, as well as my past experiences, has motivated me to become a strong team player.

I would like to begin a productive partnership with Rovinsky by meeting with you soon. I will contact you by the 25th to arrange a meeting. If you'd like to talk in the meantime, I can be reached during the work day at 555-3888 or 555-4322. I appreciate your time.

Sincerely,

Matt Bryan

Jewell Dolce
1201 Poplar Bluff Rd.
Hollywood, FL 33022
954-555-9278

March 30, 1998

Roger Heddison
Director of Public Affairs
Eastwood Mall
1111 Pine Way
Pembrooke Pines, FL 33022

Dear Mr. Heddison:

I was excited to read in the *Pembrooke Pines Reporter* that you want to install murals in all the public areas of the Eastwood Mall and plan to hire a full-time muralist for the project's duration. What a wonderful idea! I am graduating from Florida Atlantic University in six weeks and would like to be considered for the muralist position.

I will graduate with a fine arts degree and an art history minor. I have painted several murals in private homes, and have assisted in a mural project for the Pine Glen Retirement Home. I am therefore not only a talented artist, but a well-trained and disciplined one as well. My work was recently chosen as Best in Show in my university's juried student art exhibition.

My professors have praised my ability to originate new ideas and communicate them graphically. In mural painting, the ability to interpret rough sketches and verbal instructions to produce creative artwork is paramount, and those who've commissioned my murals have cited that ability in me. I possess the ability to visualize and evaluate finished products, weigh aesthetic alternatives, and make tasteful choices. My painting classes have provided me with a firm grasp of the painting process, budget limitations, and the best tools, materials, and techniques for mural painting.

I am confident that my designs will satisfy community tastes. I have some ideas for creating murals that capture events in local history, depicting little-known details and local lore.

Please allow me the opportunity to show you my portfolio of photos of my mural projects, as well as of my many student art projects. I will contact the mall office next Friday to arrange a time to meet.

Thank you for taking the time to consider me for this position.

Sincerely,

Jewell Dolce

Beth Duncan
159 Roger Williams Blvd.
Providence, RI 02903
401-555-9199

June 15, 1998

Alyssa Corday
President
GraphiCom/RI
1992 River Street
Providence, RI 02903

Dear Ms. Corday:

My comprehensive understanding of production for printed materials gained from my coursework in graphic design and digital arts at the Rhode Island School of Design qualifies me well for the graphic designer position that was recently posted on the GraphiCom/RI Web site. Along with my resume, I'm sending you some recent work and print samples.

Before my graduation last month, I interned at a local ad agency and took many projects from concept to final output. I've designed and produced posters, newsletters, and logos with little supervision.

My current position as a Web designer on the RISD campus requires me to keep a meticulous eye on detail, monitor changing technology, and support art directors on concepts and final production. My interest in design, for both print and new media, has been longstanding. I am confident that, with my education and experience, I can meet the needs of your company and clients.

I would welcome an opportunity to discuss this position and my qualifications with you in person. I will contact you in the next week to schedule an appointment. I can be reached at 401-555-9199. If I am not available, please leave a message and I will return your call promptly.

Thank you for your time and consideration. I look forward to sharing more of my design samples with you.

Sincerely,

Beth Duncan

Lee Shaw
Campus P.O. 9295
University of California at Berkeley
Berkeley, CA 94704
510-555-2659

November 25, 1998

Rebecca Rousseau
Artistic Director
StoryDance Theater Company
491 Old Bay Road
Redwood City, CA 94063

Dear Ms. Rousseau:

  You would have to look far and wide to find someone who could bring as much enthusiasm and creativity as I could to the position of assistant creative director of StoryDance. Ever since I attended StoryDance's performances as a young child, I've had a vision of the kind of creativity and energy I could add to the program.

  I carried that vision all the way to college, where I majored in theater and minored in dance. I've also taken some courses in child psychology and early education that could be instrumental in my mission to spark the creative minds and expressive movements of young children. For my senior project, I interpreted the gamut of human experience in my one-woman show, "A Woman's Work."

  My education has prepared me to teach young people about expressing characters and emotion through voice and body language, using their bodies to tell a story, and tapping into their creativity to develop material and perform with originality. I also possess the objectivity and insight to critique performances constructively and turn performing into an enriching learning experience for young people.

  I know the job entails more than just creative pursuits, and my work in summer stock has acquainted me with such tasks as locating and obtaining props, building sets, constructing costumes, applying makeup, developing special effects, managing the box office, and keeping accounts.

  Ms. Rousseau, I'd like to ask if I may meet with you to review my accomplishments and qualifications. To that end, I will phone next week to schedule an interview. I thank you most kindly for your consideration of me for this exciting position.

Cordially,

Lee Shaw

Maria Becker
University of Texas
Austin, TX 78712
512-555-9217

February 4, 1998

Ruth Starke
Principal
Sunnyside Elementary School
111 Sunny Street
Waco, TX 76798

Dear Ms. Starke:

   My enthusiastic personality, my teaching experience, and my desire to help children succeed make me the first-grade teacher you are seeking. I am interested in becoming a permanent member of your teaching staff so that together we can make a positive difference in the lives of the students at the Sunnyside School.

   My degree in early childhood and elementary education comes from the University of Texas. I have gained many diverse experiences with children in and outside the classroom, which I am convinced will make my transition into this position a successful one.

   In the six months since graduation, I have served as a substitute and have just completed a long-term substitute assignment. I understand the level of professionalism and dedication required to be effective in this field. My background and enthusiasm will provide the students with a highly competent teacher who will do what it takes to make their first-grade year a success.

   Because of my experience with computers, as well as my skill in using the Internet, I am positive I can help implement your school's new technology education program. In addition, I can assist the special education staff with the Project Early Success program in first grade because I have worked with inclusion students, as both a practicum teacher and as an aide.

   I am eager to talk with you about how my qualifications match your requirements. Knowing that the position must be filled soon, I will call you in a few days. Or, if you agree upon reviewing my letter and resume that I am the teacher you need, please call me at the phone number listed above. Thank you for your time and consideration.

Sincerely,

Maria Becker

Rachel Aguilero
Box RC-105
University of Idaho
Moscow, ID 82843
208-555-6645

March 18, 1998

Dr. Patricia Radner
Boise School District
10005 Route 31
Boise, Idaho 83707

Dear Dr. Radner:

   Having been previously employed as a substitute teacher in the Boise school district, and a graduate of Boise Central High School, I am very familiar with the school system. A soon-to-be graduate of the University of Idaho with a Bachelor of Arts degree in secondary education, I could have a positive impact as a secondary-level history teacher.

   I have four years' work and volunteer experience in the Moscow district. This past year, I worked as a teacher assistant and a youth motivator for students at risk of dropping out of school. I have worked with numerous Head Start groups in which fun and learning are interwoven. My experiences in many difficult but rewarding situations have taught me how important a motivated teacher can be.

   In addition to my work in Moscow, I have also worked in the Boise district as a substitute teacher for various grade levels. As a secondary education major, I have taken numerous courses that have prepared me with the communication and interpersonal skills crucial to teaching adolescents. My courses in history, social deviance, criminology, mass society, gender, and race and society have allowed me to place myself in other people's shoes and to understand all aspects of a situation.

   I would like to meet with you to discuss the high school–level history positions available in the Boise district. I will call in one week to set up a meeting. If you need to reach me within that time, please call me at 208-555-6645.

Sincerely,

Rachel Aguilero

Claudia Caldwell
1044 Crocus Road
Knoxville, TN 37950
615-555-8284

June 22, 1998

Dr. Perry Bartman
Research Analyst
VetMed Research, Inc.
103 Williams Parkway
Nashville, TN 37202

Dear Dr. Bartman:

As a lifelong animal lover, I was touched and inspired to read about VetMed's recent success with medications to alleviate arthritis in dogs. I am extremely excited that, as a soon-to-be graduate in biology from the University of Tennessee, I can soon make my mark in the world of veterinary pharmaceutical research. I would like to contribute to the research and development team at VetMed.

My schooling has trained me well for this work. I have co-authored several papers with my professor, Dr. Mark Whitfield, who, as you know, is a leader in the field. I am highly skilled in laboratory procedures and preparing biological specimens for study. As a communications minor, I have highly developed verbal and written skills and am unusually adept at writing up research findings.

I have engaged in complex field studies of wildlife every summer since the end of high school and have meticulously gathered and recorded data. Inspired by Dr. Whitfield, I have shifted my focus in my last two years to domesticated animals, which were the subject of my senior research project.

I am excited about sharing with you my enthusiasm for laboratory work with small animals and the contribution I know I can make in VetMed's research and development department. I intend to call you as a follow-up to this letter and schedule a meeting. You may also reach me at 615-555-8284.

Cordially,

Claudia Caldwell

Brett Atherton
1055 K Street
Brooklyn, NY 11201
718-555-2184

July 23, 1998

Dr. Davina Page
Director of Special Research
PolyChem Research, Inc.
99 118th Street
Garden City, NY 11530

Dear Dr. Page:

I would like to use my exceptional knowledge of polymers to make a valuable contribution in the polymer chemistry research lab at PolyChem. I am a recent graduate of Polytechnic University, where I received a Bachelor of Science degree in chemistry and won a national undergraduate research prize for my paper, "Effectiveness and Physical/Chemical Compatibility of Plastics Additives."

While at Polytechnic, I studied under the late Dr. Ralph Holm, who frequently suggested that my skills and research interests would be a good fit at PolyChem.

All of my professors have consistently cited my superlative abilities in the lab, and I have excelled academically. I have also worked hard to develop the kind of communication skills that enable me to translate my research into writing, as well as present the findings to other scientists. I served as president of the student chapter of the American Chemical Society and was active in numerous campuswide volunteer and community-action projects.

Obviously, there is only so much I can convey about my laboratory background and interests in this letter, so I would very much welcome the opportunity to make my case in person. Please expect a follow-up call from me in ten days so that we can schedule a meeting. I can be reached during business hours at 718-555-0284, and my voicemail can take your message if I'm not available. I look forward to meeting with you and thank you for your consideration.

Sincerely,

Brett Atherton

5783 Bonney Meadow Dr.
Phoenix, MD 21131
443-555-5398 (Phone and Fax)
mroberts@tows.edu
http://www.tows.edu/~mroberts/resource.html

September 16, 1998

Dr. Paul A. James
Chief Investigator
Queensland Pharmaceuticals, Inc.
200 State Highway 20
Gaithersburg, MD 20877

Dear Dr. James:

I am in search of a job that will put my education to the grindstone.

Because I'm always coming up with creative ideas in my field of biochemistry, I seek an opportunity to enhance the success of a team that's working on new products, ideas, and challenging research.

Since graduating Towson State College with a Bachelor of Science degree in biochemistry, I have taken graduate courses at the University at Maryland, where my advisor, Ken Germane, said I was the "best first-year student" the school had and that he was very pleased with the quality of my lab work. I can make my greatest contribution in the lab, and I want to continue this kind of productive work.

I've worked in a number of labs in the past few years, ranging from two separate labs at my undergraduate college doing independent research on breast cancer, to a summer job at Westwood-Squibb Pharmaceuticals doing analytical chemistry with medicinal patches, to working in two labs at UM researching phototransduction pathway and lambda phage repressor action. I enjoyed each of these lab experiences and work effectively and productively.

There's so much more I'd like to tell you about my experience. I would be pleased to discuss my qualifications and learn more about the opportunities available through a personal or phone interview. I will contact you in the very near future to schedule a time to meet. Please feel free to give me a call and visit my Web page, which I'm sure will answer many of your questions.

I look forward to meeting with you. Thank you for your time and consideration.

Sincerely,

Melissa Roberts

38 Glenwood Road
Omaha, NE 68105
402-555-2934

July 30, 1998

Roberta Rogers
Research Manager
Petty Research Inc.
405 County Highway 11
Lincoln, NE 68588

Dear Ms. Rogers:

A solid and successful record of research in a university agricultural lab and in the field qualifies me perfectly for the agricultural research officer position you have advertised in the *Weekend Nebraskan*.

I have spent the past four and a half years studying agricultural science at the University of Nebraska and have recently graduated. During my college years, I studied a range of subjects, including field experimentation, plant production, and crop and pasture production. The attached transcript demonstrates the excellent results I achieved in these subjects. I also conducted agronomic research trials, such as one studying the effect of sowing time on the growth of lupins, and the effect that various periods of shade had on the growth of radishes.

My written and verbal communication skills are exemplary. Throughout the course I was required to give seminars on various topics, including most recently "Plant Responses to Elevated Carbon Dioxide," for which I earned a top grade. In 1997, I achieved a Certificate of Excellence in recognition for high achievement in presentation skills.

Throughout my coursework I have gained practical farm experience on a number of properties, including a sheep property, beef property, organic property, and a dairy ranch. I learned about various types of crops (wheat, oats, lucerne, ryecorn, triticale, barley, safflower, chickpeas and linseed) and pasture systems (ryegrass and white clover, and barley grass).

I have developed a high level of computer literacy, and am familiar with both PCs and Macintoshes, as well as the major word processing and spreadsheet systems. I have had experience with computer crop modeling systems.

I am a hard worker and adapt well to various situations. I would like to request an interview and will be in touch with you in ten days to arrange an appointment. You may also reach me or by phoning or faxing 402-555-2934, where an answering machine can take your message if I'm not available.

Yours truly,

Brenda Bertram

Ashley Chang
Hunter College
New York, NY 10021
212-555-9294

Math Major

April 2, 1998

Marshall Young
Chief Executive Officer
Young, Glomar, and O'Rourke Associates
1116 Avenue of the Americas
New York, New York 10036

Dear Mr. Young:

I'm writing to tell you that I'm not just another bean counter but a bright and eager math major poised to deliver value to Young, Glomar, and O'Rourke as a financial analyst.

I will receive my Bachelor of Science degree in mathematics shortly, and I am convinced that my background matches your needs for a financial analyst. The job description indicates that financial analysts at Young, Glomar, and O'Rourke must be able to interact with clients, handle a heavy workload, prioritize and complete work under strict deadlines, work as part of a team, and work with spreadsheet and valuation programs. Here's how my background stacks up:

- Although I achieved excellent grades, I did not spend my college years as a "math geek." I was active in numerous campus organizations, honing excellent social and interpersonal skills.
- I was responsible for financing my own college education, and I proved my willingness to handle a heavy workload by working two or more jobs during much of my college career.
- My former employers and professors can tell you that I thrive under deadline pressure, never miss a due date, and always produce accurate results.
- I have worked with a wide variety of spreadsheet and valuation programs.

I would welcome the opportunity to meet with you to further explore the fit between my qualifications and the financial analyst position. I will follow up this letter with a phone call next week to schedule a meeting. Thank you in the meantime for considering me.

Sincerely,

Ashley Chang

Mark McCall
Grove City College
Grove City, PA 16127
412-555-6386

Physics Major

June 13, 1998

Dr. Seymour Steinberg
Director of Laboratory Analysis
The Motion Project
505 Industrial Parkway
Mt. Laurel, NJ 08054

Dear Dr. Steinberg:

I read with great interest of the work you are doing in your lab and of your need for project managers. As a new college graduate with a Bachelor of Science degree in physics and considerable lab experience, I would make an excellent project manager.

I noted the attributes you most seek in your project managers: excellent mathematical skills, extensive computer knowledge, the ability to work well as a team member, and a knack for problem-solving. Dr. Steinberg, I am happy to report that I possess all of these qualities. I carried a math and computer science minor while pursuing my degree from Grove City College and have an exceptional ability to grasp complex scientific and technical information.

Having served as student lab manager and chief research assistant to the chair of the physics department, I organized research teams, and usually served as team leader. I also developed teamwork skills as intramural chair of my social fraternity.

I am aware that The Motion Project needs project managers who can take responsibility for developing new projects, running existing ones, and raising money to fund the projects. The experience I gained during the summers I spent as a counselor at a computer camp for gifted high school students would transfer well to project management, since I oversaw the projects the campers created for a regional computer competition.

Dr. Steinberg, I'd like to show you just how at home I will be in your lab and would like to request that you interview me as a project manager for The Motion Project. I will contact you early next month to arrange a meeting.

Please accept my appreciation for your consideration of my qualifications.

Sincerely,

Mark McCall

1007 Garden Street
Apartment C-2
New Orleans, LA 70118
Phone: 504-555-7375
E-mail: garrick@tulane.edu

April 7, 1998

Heather Swedbourg
Human Resources Recruiter
ChemTek
1 Main Street
Mobile, AL 36601

Dear Ms. Swedbourg:

As a chemical engineering major with practical work experience and strong computer skills, I am confident that I would make a successful addition to your engineering team.

I will complete my Bachelor of Science in chemical engineering at Tulane University in May. The engineering program at Tulane is intensive, and I have supplemented it with a business minor and liberal arts courses to enhance my managerial and communication skills. In addition, I offer significant leadership experience, having served as class president in the college senate and as an instructor in the military. These skills will enable me to lead a project team at ChemTek and bring new products swiftly and profitably to market.

I am certain that my experience in both plant and laboratory environments would prove particularly useful in your chemical engineering position. This experience includes technical report writing, investigation of safety controls, and analysis of units such as reactors, heat exchangers, fluidized beds, and distillation columns.

I would like to further discuss my qualifications with you at your convenience and will call you soon to arrange an interview. I can be reached after 6 P.M. (Central) at 504-555-7375 or by e-mail at garrick@tulane.edu. Thank you for your consideration.

Sincerely,

Garrett Erickson

6501 Maritime Road, Apt. 106
Shaker Heights, OH 44101
440-555-7264

August 5, 1998

Patricia Oswaldo
Staffing Manager
MPA Incorporated
P.O. Box 410, State Route 48
Stonington, IL 62567
FAX 217-555-6031

Dear Ms. Oswaldo:

Both my education and work experience qualify me for the opening for a materials control analyst that you are advertising on your Web site.

While completing my degree, I have worked for the past two years for Rockwell Automation, where I have helped develop new products, coordinated supplier management teams (cross-functional teams), negotiated cost reductions, and supported both internal and external customers. My work experience and activities have helped to develop my leadership, communication, and presentation skills. I used my engineering background to effectively communicate our requirements to suppliers and to understand the development engineer's specifications.

I hold a Bachelor of Science degree in mechanical engineering from Pennsylvania State University's 3-2 engineering program, as well as a Bachelor of Arts degree in physics and engineering from Elizabethtown College.

You will find more information about my education and employment in the resume accompanying this fax. I am convinced you will find my background more than adequate to meet your requirements for the job opening.

I am available for an interview at your earliest convenience and will call you to set up a meeting. Please also feel free to call me at 440-555-7264 if I can answer any questions about my background.

Thank you for considering my qualifications.

Sincerely yours,

Harrison Josephs III

Bill Lomax
101 Bayshore Road
Montauk, NY 11954
516-555-1024

June 5, 1998

Claire Metts
Executive Vice President, Cost Analysis
Mayfield, Worthington & Metts, Inc.
Health Care Consulting Practice
595 Fifth Avenue
New York, NY 10017-1015

Dear Dr. Metts:

Through my research, I have learned that Mayfield, Worthington & Metts, Inc., is a leader in the health-care consulting field. I am highly interested in the role of research analyst, in which I can utilize my analytical skills to our mutual benefit.

I recently graduated from Miami University, having served an internship at the International Association for World Health. During my internship, I gained valuable knowledge of public health while helping to organize World Health Day. I also participated in the day-to-day operations of a nongovernmental organization, where I managed budgets and maintained client relations. This position piqued my interest in research, as well as in the business aspects of running an organization more efficiently.

In addition, my coursework has enhanced my statistical analysis skills, which are crucial to data interpretation and research, especially when analyzing problems and recommending and implementing solutions for clients within the health-care profession.

I would like to personally help others solve their managed care problems. My goal is to apply my experience in public health and hospitals to solving today's health-care problems. Recent health-care provider mergers and the challenges of competing with other providers have major implications for delivering efficient health-care to the public while attempting to minimize costs.

My skills and experience will enable me to help address these current challenges. I would like to arrange an interview to discuss trends in health-care consulting, the role of Mayfield, Worthington & Metts, Inc., as an industry leader, and the contribution I can make to this dynamic industry. I appreciate your time and consideration and will contact you to discuss this opportunity in the near future.

Sincerely,

Bill Lomax

Exercise Science Major

Lance Linaberry
Box 222994
University of Arizona
Tucson, AZ 85721
520-555-0193

April 18, 1998

Coach Spike Sanders
Phoenix Sun Kings
193 Sky Highway
Phoenix, AZ 85026

Dear Coach Sanders:

As a soon-to-be-degreed professional in the athletic training field, I am eager to provide my skills to the Sun Kings professional volleyball team in the assistant athletic trainer position you recently advertised.

I will receive my Bachelor of Science degree in exercise science, with a specialty in athletic training, from the University of Arizona in May. Team sports have always been my particular passion, and I have played on almost every kind of team you can imagine. While I am proud of some personal achievements as an athlete, I have always strived to balance my own performance with team objectives.

My college training has been rigorous, and I am confident that I have successfully developed the skills I need to function effectively on the "team behind the team"—the athletic trainers. I have spent my summers during college as an athletic camp counselor, assisting young people in their physical and social growth, organizing team activities, and helping them acquire the skills they needed to excel. In my numerous leadership positions in my social fraternity, I have used my talent for motivating others and helping them build self-confidence through success. I'd like to do the same for the Sun Kings.

I would very much like to meet with you and discuss my very relevant background. I will be in Phoenix early next month and would like to arrange to meet with you at that time. I'll call your office soon to set up a time.

Thank you for your consideration.

Sincerely,

Lance Linaberry

6122 Fernwood Dr.
Portland, OR 97202
503-555-9129

September 22, 1998

Walter Watanabe
Vice President
Western Systems Technologies
101 Shorefront Way
Seattle, WA 98101

Dear Mr. Watanabe:

I am applying for the programmer position that was advertised in *Computer News*. Working for your organization is particularly interesting to me because of the opportunity it presents to help build your new venture from the ground up.

I graduated from Winona State University in August with a Bachelor of Science in computer science and a minor in mathematics. I financed 70 percent of my education through scholarships and campus jobs. The education I have received has helped me to develop a solid background in computer science and outstanding problem-solving skills. I am experienced in programming in Pascal, Modula-2, C, and C++ under VAX/VMX systems.

While at Winona State University, I completed numerous programming projects. I am experienced in using queues, link-lists, and various simulations. I am accustomed to a fast-paced work environment in which deadlines are the priority. As a quick learner, I enjoy challenges and work hard to attain my goals. My experience as an officer of the university's Programming Club gave me valuable opportunities I used to sharpen my leadership and interpersonal skills. I demonstrated these skills by organizing the 1998 Annual Programmers Dinner, which nearly 300 people attended. I am confident that I can provide many valuable contributions to your organization's work.

I would appreciate having the opportunity to meet with you to further discuss how I could contribute to your team effort as an effective, reliable, and motivated programmer. I will call you to see if we can arrange a meeting. You can reach me at 503-555-9129. If I am not in, please leave a message on my answering machine.

Thank you for considering me.

Enthusiastically,

Wendy Perry

2525 K Street, NW, #231
Washington, DC 20037
Phone: 202-555-8386
Fax: 202-555-0178

May 13, 1998

Thomas Romano
Director of Operations
Corporation for Public Broadcasting
901 E Street, NW
Washington, DC 19984-2037

Dear Mr. Romano:

   I am applying for the position of assistant director of management information systems advertised on the JOBTRAK database on the Internet. This position seems tailor-made for my education, experience, and career interests, and I am ready to augment your organization's team with my enthusiasm, industry savvy, and work ethic.

   Through my major in management information systems, I've obtained solid training in management, microcomputers, and a wide variety of software programs and applications. As a computer engineer in Beijing ASEC Company, I implemented complex projects. I also improved my organizational ability while completing various assignments. In addition, my writing and analytical skills will contribution significantly to your company.

   My background and career goals match your job requirements well. I am confident that my professional knowledge, working experience, seriousness, and motivation will help me to perform the job effectively. I would be very interested in meeting with you to discuss how I can be assistance of your company. I will call the week of May 20 to arrange an appointment.

   Thank you for your consideration. I look forward to meeting with you soon.

Yours sincerely,

Jeffrey Wu

Brant Cleary
Box A-0721
Virginia Polytechnic Institute and State University
Blacksburg, VA 24061
540-555-8465

Information Technology Major

March 16, 1998

Regina Edwards
Regional Recruiter
Datamatic Corporation
40 Beachway Blvd.
Virginia Beach, VA 23458

Dear Ms. Edwards:

When I read your ad for a sales representative, I couldn't help noticing how well the requirements match my education, experience, and skills. I will graduate from Virginia Tech in two months with a major in information technology and a minor in marketing—a perfect combination for selling Datamatic software to the health-care industry.

To succeed as a sales rep, you have to know what the customer wants. My four years in the customer service department at Food Rite Supermarkets, which financed my college education, have provided me with valuable insights into customer needs. As an addition to the Datamatic team, I will not only strengthen the software product line, but also contribute to the success of the entire company.

As my supervisors at Food Rite can tell you, I am an organized, articulate, and self-motivated individual who always demonstrates a high level of commitment and a strong work ethic. Communication skills always have been extremely important to me, and I've displayed my ability to express myself well in working environments, according to my supervisor.

This combination of skills forms a solid foundation upon which I can make an immediate and meaningful contribution to your company. If upon reviewing my qualifications, you agree that I can advance Datamatic's plans and goals, I would be pleased to meet with you to further discuss my background. I will contact you in two weeks to arrange an interview. Should you have any questions before that time, you can reach me at 540-555-8465.

Thank you so much for considering my qualifications.

Sincerely,

Brant Cleary

Hood College
Campus Box 7914
Frederick, MD 21701
240-555-1927

April 14, 1998

Mr. Samuel Timothy
Director of College Recruiting and Development
Waycross Wineries
P.O. Box 9239
Modesto, California 95353

Dear Mr. Timothy:

   Your colleague, Jeff Irwin, suggested I contact you about a full-time position with Waycross Wineries. As a senior student expecting a Bachelor of Business Administration degree in general business from Hood College, I am ready to make a meaningful contribution to the Waycross Wineries marketing and sales team.

   Both my academic career and employment experience have prepared me well for a career with Waycross. My challenging and competitive academic program has included such unique courses as consumer behavior, channels and physical distribution, leadership seminars, and production and operation management, all of which would be particularly useful in your organization. In addition to my schooling, I have worked in the marketing department of SpringSweet Health Products, where I have enhanced my sales and marketing experience.

   My previous employers can verify that I am an enthusiastic and effective salesman. During my summers at SpringSweet, I consistently maintained the highest summer sales totals of any salesperson. In addition to my previous job experiences, my position as a member of Hood men's soccer team has provided me with significant leadership skills, as well as the ability to work well with a team.

   Because you undoubtedly realize that a letter and resume can convey only a limited sense of a person's qualifications, I believe it would be productive for us to meet in person, so I can present my credentials more completely. I will contact you in a few days to arrange a meeting. Should you wish to reach me before that, my number is 240-555-1927. Please leave a message if I am not available. I am looking forward to meeting with you.

   Thank you for your time and consideration.

Sincerely,

Richard Hughes

155 Sun Street
San Diego, CA 92138
619-555-2181

International Business Major

March 15, 1998

Norman Parks
Executive Vice President, Marketing
Comm-Net
1 Main Street
San Jose, CA 95113

Dear Mr. Parks:

As a highly qualified, bilingual individual with extensive work experience, I am applying for a marketing assistant position with Comm-Net. My communication, analytical, and interpersonal skills make me a great candidate.

Having obtained my Bachelor of Arts in international business with a concentration in Spanish from California State University, Fullerton, I have gained a solid background in global business through various courses in marketing, economics, and finance. Moreover, my previous employers can attest that I am a fast learner, very motivated, and extremely capable of taking on many tasks.

Working at Nova Publicidad, a Hispanic-oriented advertising agency, for the last year and a half has exposed me to the advertising aspect of the marketing process. The media department, in particular, allowed me to utilize my organizational and computer skills while at the same time functioning effectively as a team member.

Our team often faced various situations requiring maximum efficiency to reach a common goal. Effective teamwork sometimes meant producing a thirty-page presentation on an extremely tight deadline, and at other times meant developing an entire media plan for a new client from the initial research and analysis to the final suggested media plan.

My personal and professional background can make me an invaluable asset to CommNet, and I am ready to contribute to your company. I will contact you next week to set up an appointment to meet and discuss how my background would best fit your needs. If you have any questions in the meantime, please call or e-mail me at gwengoo@aol.com. Thank you for your time and consideration.

Sincerely,

Gwendolyn Goodwin

Peter Lubot
Box 9238
Haverford College
Haverford, PA 19041
215-555-1830

April 16, 1998

Ms. Ruth Williams
Senior Vice President, Operations
International Products, Inc.
28273 Vine Street
Philadelphia, PA 19106

Dear Ms. Williams:

My goal is to provide a medium-to-large multinational corporation with my hands-on experience in the international arena. Specifically, I seek a management career in international operations, international sales, or international distribution.

I will graduate from Haverford College in December. I will receive a Bachelor of Business Administration degree, specializing in management. I lived in Mexico for approximately four years, and my knowledge of Latin American cultures is quite good. I am fluent in Spanish and have a minor in that field of study.

Having undergone four years in a demanding curriculum, I am confident that I will succeed. My strategic decision-making ability, strong work ethic, and commitment toward my goals comprise only a fraction of what I have to offer International Products. I have conducted numerous research projects on the feasibility of investing in the global market. Further, I have excelled in several courses in international business and management.

I am certain that it would be of interest for both of us to meet as soon as possible. I will contact you in ten days to arrange a meeting. You can reach me at 215-555-5213.

Thank you very much for your time and consideration.

Very truly yours,

Peter Lubot

Kelly Lamar
Campus P.O. Box 102
Pine Valley University
Pine Valley, PA 19272
215-555-8123

April 12, 1998

Darcy Kettering
Customer Relations Manager
BrightStar Catalog Sales
1993 S. Broad Street
Philadelphia, PA 19148-2216

Dear Ms. Kettering:

My extensive background in customer relations, coupled with my comprehensive marketing training, will enable me to make a valuable contribution in the position of assistant director of customer relations that you are currently advertising.

Quality customer service is a basic function of my everyday life. Virtually all my employment history has required me to exercise clear, concise communication skills and to promote customer satisfaction. I have especially implemented these skills in my position as a server in a successful Pine Valley restaurant.

I will graduate from Pine Valley University with a Bachelor of Business Administration degree in marketing and a minor in information technology. My academic courses have required me to develop a vast knowledge of all the MS Office applications, the Internet, and the spreadsheet and database software programs listed in your ad. I have successfully completed numerous projects using database, spreadsheet, word processing, and desktop publishing programs.

With these skills, I an confident I am a perfect match for the customer relations position. I am most eager to implement my experience and contribute to your growing Philadelphia company. I am convinced it would be worthwhile for us to meet. I will call you soon to schedule an interview. If you have any questions, feel free to call me at 215-555-8123.

Thank you for considering me for the assistant director of customer relations position.

Cordially,

Kelly Lamar

Christian J. Raines
2020 Fern Glen Road
Spokane, WA 99258
509-555-3585

November 21, 1998

Mr. Thomas Wellington
Senior Portfolio Analyst
Wellington Portfolio Research, Inc.
P.O. Box 629501
Spokane, WA 99258

Dear Mr. Wellington:

   Your recent advertisement for a junior portfolio manager sparked my interest and seems well suited to both my experience and educational background. I will receive a Bachelor of Business Administration degree in finance from Gonzaga University in December. Throughout my academic career, I not only acquired the necessary skills to prepare me for a career in investments, but also hands-on experience in portfolio management. Coupling my education with my experience, I know I have the background to succeed in this position.

   Through participation in Gonzaga University's investments program, I have had the opportunity to take part in investment decision-making processes. Using innovative models to select and monitor stocks has given me the analytical ability to work with computer generated information in a high-tech environment. I look forward to the opportunity to apply my academic background to produce real-world results within your company.

   Thank you for your time and consideration. I can be reached at your earliest convenience by mail or telephone at 509-555-3585. As a follow-up to this letter, I will contact you within two weeks to discuss this opportunity further. Thank you for your attention.

Sincerely,

Christian J. Raines

1360 Ferry Street Apt. #55
Portland, OR 97401
503-555-4413

September 22, 1998

Arthur Pollack
Chairman
Pollack, McKnight & Fritz
9192 Spring View Terrace
Eugene, OR 97401

Dear Mr. Pollack:

I am interested in speaking with you regarding a junior accountant position with Pollack, McKnight & Fritz.

I will receive my Bachelor of Science degree in accounting this December from Reed College, graduating *summa cum laude*. I am confident that the combination of my strong educational background and practical work experience has prepared me to make an immediate contribution to Pollack, McKnight & Fritz.

Having been awarded the Institute of Internal Auditors Award, inducted into the National Honor Society for Business, and maintained a successful small business, I understand the commitment and professionalism required for success in the accounting field.

I would very much appreciate the opportunity of a personal interview, at your convenience, to further discuss my abilities and the needs of Pollack, McKnight & Fritz, and I will call you in two weeks to arrange a meeting.

Thank you for considering me.

Sincerely,

Timothy Rickman

1545 Pueblo Avenue
San Jose, CA 95113
408-555-7192

20 November 1998

Jack Marshall
Director of Public Relations
Springtime Industries
505 Haymarket St.
San Diego, CA 92138

Dear Mr. Marshall:

When I spoke with you at Frank and Mary Sue Rawlinson's Fourth of July cookout, I thought about what an interesting person you would be to work for. I was very excited when Frank suggested that I apply for the position you will have available in the public relations department in the spring of 1999. It would be wonderful to work for your prestigious company.

I know that you need someone who is enthusiastic and task-oriented, and I am uniquely qualified for the job. Some people are great team performers, while others are better working on their own—I am both!

My experiences working at Santa Fe River National Bank and as the supervisor of the San Jose State University admissions telemarketing crew convey that I am a successful group worker and team leader, while my experience as historian of my fraternity proves that I can organize events and keep excellent records on my own. I am fluent in Spanish, which is imperative to your company's work in Southern California. I also have proficient computer skills, as I work daily with the Microsoft Office programs and the Internet.

As you can see, I am a dynamic person with great interest in your company. My campus and extracurricular work have provided me with the skills to be an asset to your company. My outgoing personality, accompanied by my profit- and task-oriented character, makes me an excellent choice for the job.

I will contact your secretary this week for an interview. I look forward to speaking with you again soon, and I thank you for your time and consideration.

Sincerely,

Ted Tarnower

Tiffany Smithfield
909 Betton Hills Road
Tallahassee, FL 32308
850-555-9217

March 29, 1998

Joyce Canova
Editor, *DataView*
Data Publications
1149 Seaview Blvd.
Pensacola, FL 32502

Dear Ms. Canova:

I have a wealth of skills and talents to offer in the editorial assistant position you currently have open. I will graduate in July with a Bachelor of Arts degree in communications from Florida State University, and I am eager to put my attributes to work for you at *DataView* magazine.

Let me describe what sets me apart from other candidates:

- Because I minored in computer science, I have a knack for expressing complex subject matter in easily understood language.
- I conducted several projects while in school that won high marks for design. I've been told that my layouts are memorable and attractive to readers.
- I was the technology editor for the 30,000-circulation campus daily, *The Florida Flambeau*, for two years.
- I'm a meticulous proofreader; I have a firm grasp of English grammar and syntax and can catch errors easily. My classmates often ask me to review their papers.

I know you won't regret talking to me about this position. I'm eager to bring samples of my work to an interview. I will give you a call early next month to set up a meeting. You can reach me at 850-555-9217 in the meantime.

Thank you for considering me.

Sincerely,

Tiffany Smithfield

PART SIX

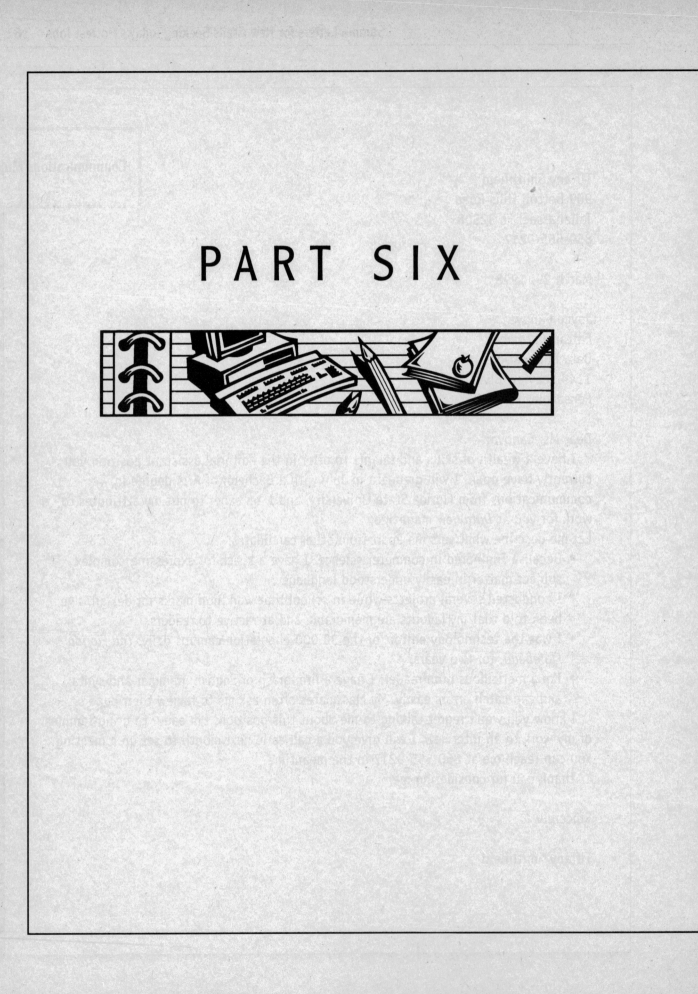

Letters for Graduate and Professional School Grads

One substantial difference between the cover letters of graduate and professional school students and those of undergraduates is the greater likelihood that graduate school grads will employ networking techniques. Professionals leaving graduate school may also need to incorporate into their cover letters any experience they've garnered in the time between their baccalaureate degree and graduate degrees.

At the doctorate level, a significant number of graduates pursue advanced degrees because they are interested in university teaching or research. Doctoral students seeking to enter academia frequently don't even write their own cover letters; instead, their major professor writes a letter of introduction for them. But once students have their doctorates in hand and are out of the degree-granting institution, they write their own cover letters to colleges and universities with teaching vacancies. In academia, the curriculum vitae replaces the resume, and unlike in the rest of the job-seeking world, brevity is not especially valued. In fact, the longer your curriculum vitae, the more likely you are to land a position. Similarly, Ph.D.'s have a bit of license to write lengthy cover letters. Thus, in this chapter, you'll find this book's only example of a two-page cover letter.

John Randall
535 Peachtree Parkway
Atlanta, GA 30301
404-555-8273

August 17, 1998

Jennifer Rigsby, Esq.
Riley Hoyt Valderama Rigsby Parsons & King, P.C.
150 Skyline Way
Atlanta, GA 30301

Dear Ms. Rigsby:

   Bart Whitfield suggested I contact you about openings for associates at your firm. The combination of my extensive education and experience offer me the unique opportunity to make a positive contribution to Riley Hoyt Valderama Rigsby Parsons & King, P.C. As you review my resume, you will find my experience and education commensurate with a position as a criminal attorney.

   I graduated from Emory University School of Law, where I received a J.D. I also hold an M.B.A. and a Certificate in International Business, which I earned at Emory. I recently passed the Georgia State Bar Examination.

   The skills I have acquired outside the classroom have augmented my academic experience. At the DeKalb County Prosecutor's Office I have been involved in all facets of investigations. Perhaps my most exciting experience was being assigned to the sensitive Organized Crime Unit, a responsibility that indicated the tremendous faith and trust the office placed in me.

   Most recently, through appellate practice, I have been able to hone my skills in writing, creative thinking, oral argument and presentation, and most importantly, research and analysis. Moreover, having worked in a law enforcement environment, I respect the value and necessity of teamwork, honesty, and mutual trust and support.

   I would certainly like to put my skills, experience, and education to work for Riley Hoyt Valderama Rigsby Parsons & King, P.C. I would welcome the opportunity to meet with you to discuss my employment potential. I plan to contact you in two weeks to arrange a meeting. I can be reached at 404-555-1302.

   Thank you for your consideration. I look forward to meeting with you.

Sincerely,

John Randall

Mark Titus
1505 Commonwealth Avenue
Roanoke, VA 24022
540-555-6263

August 15, 1998

Christine Lennard
James Madison Legal Research Group
P.O. Box 8283
Williamsburg, VA 23185

Dear Ms. Lennard:

   I understand from your associate Margy Orth that you are seeking someone to join your Public Law team. I have recently passed the Bar, having graduated from University of Virginia Law School, and would be most interested in speaking with you about your plans for this position. My law school performance was exemplary. My accomplishments include selection for the school's National Appellate Advocacy Team, successful representation before an administrative law judge, and a summer fellowship with Fox Hollow Legal Services.

   My interest in public law and the process of governing motivated me to attend law school. My curriculum included a concentration in environmental law with its heavy emphasis on administrative law; I also took a course in state and local government and another in advanced legal research. My undergraduate work included service as a student member of the University Judicial Board. I attended hearings, was involved in appeals, prepared documentation, and participated in conducting investigations.

   I would welcome the opportunity to join your organization. I will call you in a few days to determine if I might schedule an appointment to meet with you.

   Thank you for your time and consideration.

Sincerely,

Mark Titus

Master's of Business
Administration (M.B.A.)
Graduate

1404 Natchez Rd.
Nashville, TN 37240
615-555-1429
E-mail: NC.Nat@vandy1998.com

July 13, 1998

Ms. Sally Mulcahy
HR Director
Staffing Dept. 114
PO Box 18840-B
Phoenix, AZ 85072

Dear Ms. Mulcahy:

   Having just attained an M.B.A. degree from Vanderbilt University, I am eager to apply my enhanced financial skills in the treasury analyst position available.

   I am uniquely qualified for this position. Among my qualifications and skills that meet your needs are the following:

   • Master of Business Administration degree in finance and investment valuation; Bachelor of Business Administration degree in economics.
   • Solid and well-rounded financial analysis experience, including analysis of investment alternatives.
   • Strong knowledge of markets and ERISA gleaned through CFA enrollment.
   • Excellent computer skills, highly proficient in spreadsheets, including Excel and Lotus 1-2-3.
   • Strong team player with enthusiasm and drive who is committed to the highest work ethics.

   I am confident that I can make an immediate and valuable contribution to your success. In me, you'll find someone who is unusually dedicated and efficient, with the analytical and personal skills necessary to excel in a fast-paced environment.

   I would welcome the opportunity to discuss with you further how I could meet your needs. I plan to visit Phoenix soon, and will contact you when I arrive in town to schedule an interview. I look forward to talking with you.

   Thank you for your consideration.

Sincerely,

Nathaniel Charleson

**Master's of Business
Administration (M.B.A.)
Graduate**

Ming Sun
3987 I St. NW. #194
Washington, DC 20037
202-555-1234

September 25, 1998

Gillian Fairweather
Project Director
Peregrine/Asia International Development Corporation
1844 Pennsylvania Avenue
Washington, DC 20037

Dear Ms. Fairweather:

My practical experience in international trading between China and other countries, gained through an internship with U.S.-Asia Commercial Development Corporation, can make me a genuine asset to Peregrine/Asia International Development Corporation as a trade analyst.

I have gained considerable knowledge of international business and finance through my M.B.A. studies at George Washington University. Through my experiences and academic background, I have acquired skills in many areas, including finance, research, communication, negotiation, and analysis, which can contribute to your corporation.

I am also familiar with the business environment in Asia, especially in China, knowledge that can be extremely valuable in your endeavors. I am confident that my professional knowledge, work experience, and organizational ability will help me to perform the job effectively. I would be very interested in meeting with you and discussing how I can contribute to your corporation. I will call you next week to schedule an appointment.

Thank you for your consideration. I look forward to meeting with you soon.

Sincerely yours,

Ming Sun

Jack Fischetti
411 Bayleaf Road, Apt. B-6
Wilmette, IL 60091
847-555-5286
fischetti@uchi.edu

September 12, 1997

Xavier O'Boyle
Engineering Director
Observatron Products
9999 West Boulevard
San Diego, CA 92138-0001

Dear Mr. O'Boyle:

I will receive my doctoral degree in materials science and engineering from the University of Chicago this fall and would like to bring my solid engineering background and strong skills to your firm. Because of the outstanding reputation of your company, I would welcome an opportunity to continue the firm's success in a capacity as a research scientist or development engineer.

I have a broad base of experience and, having worked in an electroceramics group, I have been introduced to a variety of materials systems. My communication and interpersonal skills are excellent and would be an asset to your company.

I would like to request the opportunity to discuss my qualifications in greater detail, and will call your secretary next week to arrange an interview. I can be reached at 847-555-5286 during the day, at 847-555-9914 in the evening, or through e-mail at fischetti@uchi.edu. If you are aware of others in the company currently in search of a young, creative research engineer, I would be most appreciative if you could provide me with their names, or alternatively, forward my credentials for their review.

Thank you for your time and consideration. I look forward to meeting with you.

Sincerely,

Jack Fischetti

June 2, 1998

Dr. Blake Reed
Human Resources Manager
Metamorphosis Pharmaceuticals, Inc.
833 Patriot's Lane
Cambridge, Massachusetts 02139

Dear Dr. Reed:

   I was pleased to read in the *Boston Sunday Globe* that you are seeking a research
associate to assist in your gene-based studies of cancer. With my experience and my
enthusiasm for scientific research, I am convinced that I will be a valuable asset to the
Metamorphosis cancer research team. I have more than four years' experience working
as a research assistant in the molecular biology laboratory of Dr. Eli Rose at St.
Bernadette's Hospital in Waltham. In my work on the cloning, characterization, and
analysis of expression of the CD18 (á2 leukocyte integrin) gene promoter, I have
become proficient in many molecular biology techniques, including:
  * nucleic acid isolation, purification, and manipulation;
  * Northern, Southern, and Western blotting;
  * PCR and RT-PCR, gene expression assays; and
  * electrophoretic mobility shift assays.
Currently I am completing a laboratory research rotation for Harvard University's
graduate program in molecular cell biology and biochemistry in Dr. Ramona Fosberry's
laboratory, investigating the mechanisms of resistance of a chronic myelogenous cell
line to apoptosis. In this work, I routinely use the following techniques:
  * tissue culture;
  * protein isolation;
  * immunoprecipitation;
  * Western blotting;
  * fluorescence microscopy; and
  * flow cytometry.
   With my knowledge, experience, and enthusiasm for scientific research, I know that I
can be a valuable asset to the Metamorphosis cancer research team. I would like to
meet with you to discuss my credentials and their application to the needs and the
continued success of Metamorphosis Pharmaceuticals. I look forward to speaking with
you soon and will call at the end of next week to schedule a time to meet. Thank you
for your consideration.

Sincerely,

Jessica Denton

Ph.D. Student Seeking
Career Change

Jared Dittmaier
1003 Benjamin Franklin Parkway
Philadelphia, PA 19102
215-555-2841

October 27, 1998

Ms. Daphne Martin
Senior Business Analyst
McKinsey & Company, Inc.
55 E. 52nd St.
New York, NY 10051

Dear Ms. Martin:

   As my graduate work at the University of Pennsylvania is close to completion, I am looking to bring my analytical, computational, and problem-solving skills to a firm like yours. I was impressed by the recent McKinsey & Company on-campus presentation, and I am very interested in teaming up with your firm as a management consultant.

   I have proven myself to be an original and incisive thinker through my research in theoretical chemistry. I also develop models from theories to address problems at hand. My ability to work out complex problems would be most advantageous to your company. Because I was born in Hong Kong, am widely traveled, and am an active participant in many international organizations, I am convinced that my cultural experiences can contribute to McKinsey's global goals.

   This combination of experience and education can make me a valuable asset to McKinsey & Company. I am eager to meet with you to discuss the opportunity to be a member of the team. I will contact you at the end of next week to see when we might meet. My home phone/fax number is 215-555-2841, and I can be reached at work at 215-555-5513.

   I greatly appreciate your consideration.

Sincerely,

Jared Dittmaier

Paul Marks
1545 South 5th Street
Pittsburgh, PA 15233
412-555-6362

August 12, 1998

Dr. Francis Mulcahy
Chair, Biology Search Committee
University of Richmond
Richmond, VA 23173

Dear Dr. Mulcahy:

   Please accept this letter and the enclosed documents as application for the assistant professor of biology position at the University of Richmond listed on *The Chronicle of Higher Education* Web site. For the past two years I have been a postdoctoral research fellow in Dr. Lois Wagner's laboratory in the Department of Molecular Genetics at All Children's Hospital. Dr. Wagner is one of the world's top experts on molecular genetic immunology.

   Over the course of my academic training, I have accomplished a unique blend of research and teaching experience that fulfills the criteria listed in your ad. As a graduate student at the University of Pittsburgh, I:

   • conducted lecture and laboratory courses in general biology,
   • coordinated an intensive immunology laboratory,
   • assisted in a physiology lecture course, and
   • implemented a bacterial protein expression section for the departmental molecular biology workshop.

   I have continued my commitment to education in my current position by directing several undergraduates in research projects in molecular biology and by teaching at Pitt Junior College. Collectively, this teaching experience provides me with practical knowledge about how to supervise effectively in both classroom and laboratory settings.

   Similarly, the diversity of my research experiences will be invaluable not only when conducting a research program, but also in providing current and pertinent topics for lecture and laboratory experiments. My doctoral research under the guidance of Dr. Russ Maffett, a leading expert in invertebrate biochemistry and physiology, focused on a fundamental question of cellular physiology and utilized a wide range of cellular and molecular techniques. My current research employs molecular protocols to identify and characterize novel immune system genes (see vitae).

I am confident that I can succeed at the University of Richmond as both a teacher and a researcher, and I ask you to seriously consider my application. My broad background in cellular and molecular biology, genetics, and physiology has given me a unique perspective, as well as the practical advantages that come with diverse experiences. This is true for research, but I think even more so for teaching. I will contact you after the search period is closed to see if I can arrange a campus visit. I look forward to discussing my candidacy with you and I extend my thanks for considering me.

Enthusiastically,

Paul Marks, Ph.D.

Resources

It is my sincere hope that this book has taught you what you need to know to create your own dynamic cover letters that will help propel you into your post-graduation career. I am always willing to answer questions and critique the cover letters of consumers of this book as well as consider suggestions, so please write or e-mail me:

Katharine Hansen
1250 Valley View Lane
DeLand, FL 32720-2364
khansen@stetson.edu

and visit the Quintessential Career and Job-Hunting Resources Guide on the World Wide Web at:

http://www.stetson.edu/~rhansen/careers.html

Knowing that cover letters are an important part of a college student's job search—but not the complete package—I recommend the following "must-have" career books for your library:

- Asher, Donald. *From College to Career.* (Berkeley, CA: Ten Speed Press, 1992. Out of print, but available in libraries.) An excellent resource about resumes for college students.

- Bolles, Richard. *What Color Is Your Parachute?* (Berkeley, CA: Ten Speed Press, updated yearly.) Covers a far broader audience than just college students, but the author's exercises for identifying career skills and interests are unbeatable. Also has excellent material about informational interviewing.

- Chapman, Jack. *How to Make $1000-a-Minute: Negotiating Your Salaries and Raises.* (Berkeley, CA: Ten Speed Press, 1996.) Chapman helps job-seekers develop effective ways to negotiate salaries.

- Combs, Patrick. *Major in Success*, revised edition (Berkeley, CA: Ten Speed Press, 1998.) A fun, accessible book that not only helps with launching your career, but also offers ideas for getting the most out of college.

- Kennedy, Joyce Lain. *Electronic Resume Revolution.* (New York: John Wiley & Sons, Inc., 1995.)

- Krueger, Brian. *College Grad Job Hunter.* (Milwaukee, WI: Quantum Leap Press, 1997.) An excellent and comprehensive resource for college

173

- Krueger, Brian. *College Grad Job Hunter.* (Milwaukee, WI: Quantum Leap Press, 1997.) An excellent and comprehensive resource for college students.

- O'Brien, Patrick. *Making College Count.* (Green Bay, WI: Graphic Management Corp., 1996.) Another good resource for getting the most out of college.

- Weinstein, Bob. *Resumes Don't Get Jobs* (New York: McGraw Hill, 1993.) Weinstein explodes numerous "myths" about job-seeking.

I wish you much success in writing dynamic cover letters. Please accept my very best wishes as you travel this important crossroads in your life!

Index

A

Academic experience
  avoiding overemphasizing, 24–26
  describing, 28, 42–48
Accounting major, sample letter for, 159
Active voice, 32
Advertised openings
  asking for resumes only, 3
  blind box, 11–12
  online, 121
  responding to, 10–12
  responding to, by e-mail, 122
  tailoring your letter to, 68–72
Agricultural science major, sample letter for, 144
Apostrophes, problems with, 32–33
Autobiography, avoiding, 77–78

B

Biochemistry major, sample letter for, 143
Biology major, sample letter for, 141
Blind box ads, 11–12
Business letter format, 33–35
Business major, sample letter for, 154

C

Career fairs, 76, 111
CareerWeb, 120
Chemical engineering major, sample letter for, 147
Chemistry major, sample letter for, 142
Clichés, avoiding, 29
Closing, 14
Closing paragraph. See Final paragraph
Cold-contact letters, 9–10, 65
College. See Academic experience; Graduate school

College career placement office, 98–99
Communication skills, 3, 49
Communications major, sample letter for, 161
Computer science major, sample letter for, 151
Confidence, lack of, 57
Coursework, 28, 42–43
Cover letters. See also Sample letters
  closing, 14
  faxing, 37
  final paragraph, 13–14, 15–16, 60–61
  focusing, 77–79
  formats, 20–22, 33–35
  handwritten, 36
  length of, 17
  mailing, 38
  most common mistakes in, 14–19
  opening paragraph, 12–13, 17, 27, 54–57
  original meaning of, 1
  paper for, 36
  postscripts to, 22
  producing, 36
  purposes of, 2–3
  quantifying and exemplifying in, 8–9
  referral, 12, 56, 73–77
  resumes and, 2–3, 18–19
  salary requirements in, 17, 30–31
  salutation, 11, 12, 14, 18, 33, 76
  signature, 27, 33
  structure, 12–14
  tailoring to a want ad, 68–72
  types of, 9–12
  used to differentiate yourself from other job-seekers, 4–9
  what not to include, 29
  what to include, 27–29
  when to send, 3
  without resumes, 103–4

E

Elementary education major, sample
    letter for, 139
E-mail, 38, 122, 123
Employers
    blind box ads used by, 11–12
    demonstrating knowledge of,
        18, 64–67
    emphasizing what you can do
        for, 61–64
    getting attention of, 20–24
    point of view of, 7, 16, 31
English major, sample letter for, 126
Entrepreneurial skills, 51
Entry-level jobs, 4, 17
E-Span, 120
Exercise science major, sample letter
    for, 150
Experience
    academic, 24–26, 28, 42–48
    lack of, 17–18
    transferable work, 48–53
Externships, 82, 92
Extracurricular activities, 28, 43, 46

F

Faxing, 37
Field of study, proficiency in, 50
Final paragraph, 13–14, 15–16, 60–61
Finance major, sample letter for, 158
Follow-up letters, 105–15
    to accept a job offer, 114
    to decline a job offer, 114–15
    after rejection, 112–14
    thank-you letters after interviews,
        105–12
Fonts, 36
Foreign languages major, sample letter
    for, 127
Formats, 20–22, 33–35

G

Geography major, sample letter for, 135
GPA, 28
Graduate school
    letters to accompany application to,
        115–17

Graduate students
    seeking career change, 170
    seeking college teaching job, 171–72
    seeking medical research position, 169
    seeking position in industry, 168
Graduation date, 28–29
Graphic design major, sample letter
    for, 137

H

Handwritten letters, 36
Health major, sample letter for, 149
History major, sample letter for, 133
Human resources department, 11

I

Informational interviews, 73–74, 75,
    95–97
Information technology major, sample
    letter for, 153
International business major, sample letter
    for, 155
International relations major, sample letter
    for, 132
Internet job hunting, 119–23
Internships, 16, 74, 76, 82, 83–91
Interpersonal skills, 49
Interviews
    asking for, 2, 13–14, 56, 60–61
    following up rejection after, 112–14
    informational, 73–74, 75, 95–97
    sending thank-you letters after, 105–12

J

Job listings, online, 121
Job offers
    accepting, 114
    declining, 114–15

K

Keywords, 21, 37–38
Kitchen Sink paragraphs, 78–79

L

Law school graduate, sample letters
for, 164–65
Leadership skills, 49–50
Letterhead, 33
Letters. *See also* Cover letters; Sample
letters
of recommendation, 29
standard business format, 33–35

M

Mailing, 38
Mail-merge, 10
Management information systems major,
sample letter for, 152
Management major, sample letter for, 156
Marketing major, sample letter for, 157
Mass mailings, 10
Math major, sample letter for, 145
M.B.A. graduate, sample letters for,
166–67
Mechanical engineering major, sample
letter for, 148
Mission statements, 67
Mistakes, most common, 14–19
Monster Board, 120

N

Networking, 73–77
Newsgroups, 122–23
Nontraditional students, 7

O

Occupational Outlook Handbook, 30
Online Career Center, 120
On-the-job learning, 59
Opening paragraph, 12–13, 17, 27,
54–57
Overqualified, appearing, 71

P

Paper, 36
Passive voice, 32
PEP formula, 7–8, 16, 61
Performing arts major, sample letter
for, 138

Personality, opening a window into
your, 23–24
Ph.D. students. *See* Graduate students
Philosophy major, sample letter for, 128
Physics major, sample letter for, 146
Pinpoint Salary Service, 30
Political science major, sample letter
for, 134
Positive, accentuating the, 57–59
Postscripts, 22
Printers, 36
Profitability, Efficiency, and Productivity
formula. *See* PEP formula
Psychology major, sample letter for, 129
Public relations major, sample letter
for, 160

Q

Quintessential Career and Job-Hunting
Resource Guide, 120

R

Record keeping, 38–39
Recruiters, 100–102, 112
Referral cover letters, 12, 56, 73–77
Rejection, following up after, 112–14
Religious studies major, sample letter
for, 131
ResumePATH, 121
Resumes
cover letters and, 2–3, 18–19
databases of, 120–21
scanning, 3, 37
sending letters without, 103–4

S

Salary requirements, 17, 30–31
Salutation, 11, 12, 14, 18, 33, 76
Sample letters
to accompany graduate school
application, 116–17
to college career placement office, 99
to college recruiters, 101–2
following up after rejection, 112–14
for graduate and professional school
students, 163–72
for internships, externships, and
summer jobs, 82–94

Sample letters, *continued*
  for new grads by major, 125–61
  requesting informational interviews,
    96–97
  sent without resumes, 103–4
  standard business format, 34–35
  thank-you letters, 107–14
  using, 125
Scanning, 37–38
Secondary education major, sample letter
  for, 140
Sentence structure
  checking, 31
  varying, 19
Sexism, avoiding, 18
Signature, 27, 33
Skills
  communication, 3, 49
  entrepreneurial, 51
  leadership, 49–50
  teamwork and interpersonal, 49
  transferable, 48–53
Sociology major, sample letter for, 130
Structure, 12–14
Summer jobs, 71, 74, 76, 82, 93–94

T

Teamwork skills, 49
Thank-you letters
  after interviews, 105–12
  after rejections, 112–14

Titles, use of, 33
Transcripts, 28

U

Unique Selling Proposition (USP), 4–7,
  20, 22
Usenet, 122–23

V

Verbs, choice of, 32, 58
Visual arts major, sample letter for, 136

W

Want ads. *See* Advertised openings
Web sites
  creating your own, 122
  on informational interviewing, 74
  on salaries, 31
  for submitting cover letters, 120, 121
Work-ethic traits, 50
Work-study, 43, 45
Writing samples, 29
Writing style, 31–33
  active, descriptive verbs, 32, 58
  apostrophe problems, 32–33
  avoiding clichés, 29
  avoiding overblown language, 59
  avoiding overuse of "I," 19
  conciseness of, 31
  sharpening your focus, 77–79

Katharine Hansen

KATHARINE HANSEN is a writer and instructor at Stetson University, DeLand, Florida. Her previous books are *Dynamic Cover Letters* and *Write Your Way to a Higher GPA*, written with Randall S. Hansen and published by Ten Speed Press. Hansen was writer-editor at numerous newspapers, magazines and nonprofit organizations, and she served as speechwriter for the first woman elected to the Florida Cabinet. Hansen, who received her bachelor of arts degree in humanities from Stetson University, lives in DeLand with her writing partner, Randall, children, Mary and John, and two retired racing greyhounds.